Building Pembroke chapel:

Wren, Pearce and Scott

A.V. Grimstone

Pembroke College, Cambridge

All rights reserved. No part of this publication may be reproduced, transmitted, or stored in a retrieval system, in any form or by any means, without prior permission in writing from the publisher and the author of this book.

Copyright © A V Grimstone, 2009

First published by Pembroke College, Cambridge, 2009

Designed and composed by Beate Alldis, Willowprint Services Ltd
Set in Minion Pro
Printed in England by BAS Fine Art Printers, Amesbury, Wiltshire

ISBN 978-0-9563213-0-5

*Old houses were scaffolding once
and workmen whistling.*

T E Hulme

CONTENTS

List of illustrations — viii
Photograph credits — ix
Acknowledgements — x
Abbreviations — x
Preface — xi

Prologue — 1

INTRODUCTION — 3

THE DONOR AND HIS GIFT: MATTHEW WREN — 6

THE SEVENTEENTH-CENTURY CHAPEL

THE PRESENT BUILDING — 16

PERSONALIA — 20
    Christopher Wren — 20
    Edward Pearce — 24

CONTEXT — 27

DESIGN: STAGES AND SOURCES — 29
    The preliminary drawing — 29
    The model — 39
    Sources — 45
    Dimensions — 52

THE VAULT — 55

THE EXTERIOR   59
   Brickwork: the side elevations   59
   The west and east façades   61
   Stone carving   63

THE INTERIOR   71
   The ante-chapel and organ loft   71
   The chapel: overall plan   73
   Woodwork and wood-carving: the body of the chapel   75
   Woodwork and wood-carving: the east end   91
   Plasterwork   101
   Paving   106

THE CLOISTER AND THE VESTRY   109

CONSECRATION   112

CONCLUSION   113
   Comparison with Emmanuel College chapel   113
   Edward Pearce   116

POSTSCRIPT:
GEORGE GILBERT SCOTT'S EXTENSION   121

APPENDICES   129
   Appendix 1: The burials in the vault   129
   Appendix 2: The Pembroke Old Library   130
   Appendix 3: Stained glass: the twentieth century   132

BIBLIOGRAPHY   136

INDEX   140

List of illustrations

1. Matthew Wren's funeral procession
2. Pembroke College from Loggan's, *Cantabrigia Illustrata*
3. Matthew Wren, portrait
4. Scott's survey plan of the original chapel
5. The chapel from the north
6. Portrait of Edward Pearce, by Isaac Fuller
7. Preliminary study for the north elevation, by Edward Pearce
8. Old St Paul's cathedral, transept elevation
9. Dimensions and ratios in the preliminary drawing
10. Study for St. Edmund King and Martyr, London, by Edward Pearce
11. Dunster Castle, carved doorcase
12. Chapel model from north-west
13. Chapel model from south-east
14. Roof trusses in chapel model
15. Roof trusses in chapel model and as built
16. Pilaster base profile, from chapel model
17. Pilaster base drawing, by Wren
18. Corinthian column base, from Palladio
19. Chapel, west front
20. Serlio's elevation of the Temple of the Sibyl
21. Serlio's plan of the Temple of the Sibyl
22. Chapel, east end
23. The Queen's chapel, St James's Palace, London
24. Chapel window, north side
25. Design for window, Somerset House chapel, London, by Inigo Jones
26. Chapel cupola
27. Geometry of chapel west front
28. Survey of the vault
29. Vault interior
30. Inscription, 'EP 1665'
31. Chapel urn, wall drawing
32. Urn, after Scott's renovation
33. Urn, modern replacement
34. Urn from Loggan, *Cantabrigia Illustrata*
35. Urn on gate pier, Clare College, Cambridge
36. Urn, from engraving by Edward Pearce senior
37. Carving in the west pediment
38. Carving in west pediment, wall drawing
39. Chapel interior, looking west
40. Oculus framing, in the organ loft
41. Design for chapel stalls, by Edward Pearce
42. Stalls carving, foot
43. Emmanuel College chapel stalls carving, foot
44. Carving above the stalls
45. Cartouche, cherub type
46. Cartouche, grotesque type
47. Cherub heads, montage
48. *Book of friezes*, by Edward Pearce senior (details)
49. Auricular cartouche, by Lukas Kilian
50. Drawing of cartouche, by Edward Pearce
51. Cornelius Austin's presumed initial 'A'
52. Festoon, Emmanuel College chapel, carved by Cornelius Austin
53. Survey drawing of original chapel east end, by Scott
54. Original chapel interior, photograph
55. Carving on east end panelling (detail)
56. Carving on east end panelling

57	Reredos, as altered by Scott	73	Survey drawing of chapel north-west end exterior, by Scott
58	Pilaster capital, reredos	74	Relieving arch in chapel wall
59	Pilaster capital, west front	75	Altar rail, Emmanuel College chapel
60	Pilaster capital, study, by Edward Pearce	76	*Book of friezes*, detail, by Edward Pearce senior,
61	Capital, west end interior	77	Christopher Wren, bust, by Edward Pearce
62	Reredos drop	78	George Gilbert Scott
63	Reredos cartouche	79	Scott's original proposal for new east end, interior
64	Prayer desk	80	Chapel interior, looking east to Scott's extension
65	Communion rails	81	Old Library, bookcase end
66	Wall decoration, plasterwork	82	Old Library, carving at east end
67	Wall decoration, detail of mascaron	83	Stained glass, detail of left-hand window
68	Mascaron from *Book of friezes*, by Edward Pearce senior	84	Stained glass, the east window
69	Ceiling, general view		
70	Chapel section, from *Building News*		
71	Ceiling, detail		
72	Wren's notes on paving		

Photograph Credits

All Souls College, Oxford 8, 10, 17, 41; Ashmolean Museum, University of Oxford 77; James Austin 14, 24, 26, 55, 62, 74; James Campbell 15, 28; Conway Library, Courtauld Institute of Art, London 23; IPC Media, *Country Life* 39, 65, 80; Ian Fleming 22, 29, 30, 31, 35, 37, 42, 43, 46, 47, 52, 56, 61, 67, 71, 75, 83, 84; Guildhall Library, by permission of the Dean & Chapter of St Paul's Cathedral, London 50, 60; Christopher Hurst 45; Edward Leigh 5; ©National Monuments Record 44, 57, 58, 63, 64, 69; National Portrait Gallery/ W M Clarke 78; ©NTPL/Nadia Mackenzie 11; Pembroke College Architectural Archive 7, 32, 33, 40, 54, 66, 81, 82; Pembroke College Archives 1, 72; RIBA Library Drawings & Archives Collections 4, 25, 53, 73, 79; Rijksmuseum, Amsterdam 36, 49; Yale Center for British Art, Paul Mellon Fund 6; V and A Images, Victoria & Albert Museum, London 48, 68, 76; Paul Whitehead 12, 13; Robert Williams 51

Acknowledgements

The poem '*Image*' by T E Hulme, which appears as the epigraph, is quoted from *The life and opinions of T E Hulme,* edited by Alun R Jones (Gollancz,1960). Attempts to discover the copyright holder of this poem have been unsuccessful.

The quotation on p.90 from Douglas Bush's essay 'Science and literature', in H H Rhys (ed.), *Seventeenth century science and the arts* (1961), is reproduced by permission of Princeton University Press.

The quotation on pp.118 from *Catalogue of European sculpture in the Ashmolean Museum*, vol. 3 by Nicholas Penny (1992) is reproduced by permission of Oxford University Press.

Abbreviations

PCA	Pembroke College Archives.
PAG	Pembroke College Cambridge Society Annual Gazette.
RCHM Cambridge	Royal Commission on Historical Monuments, England, An inventory of the historical monuments in the City of Cambridge (London, 1959).
Willis and Clark	Robert Willis and John W Clark, *The architectural history of the University of Cambridge*, 4 vols (Cambridge, 1886).
Wren Society	A T Bolton and H D Hendry, (eds) *The Wren Society*, 20 vols (Oxford, 1924–43).

Preface

For a retired biologist to offer an account of the building history of what is assumed to be Christopher Wren's first architectural work can scarcely fail to seem presumptuous. In mitigation I would plead, first, that professional architectural historians have neglected the task, but secondly, that they have been remarkably generous in helping me to undertake it. The reader will find that, to a considerable extent, my role has been to act as a catalyst, persuading them to apply their knowledge to material not previously brought to their attention.

A principal finding of this study is that Edward Pearce played an important part in bringing Pembroke chapel into being. The first debt that I must gratefully acknowledge, therefore, is that to Arnold Pacey, who first suggested, informally, that Pearce may have worked at Pembroke, as a stone carver. This inspired conjecture, which Dr Pacey was himself unable to follow up, was an invaluable starting point for me and led in unexpected directions.

My chief mentor has been Gordon Higgott who, in addition to trying to educate me in seventeenth-century architectural history, has been a constant source of advice and encouragement. Directly or indirectly, he is responsible for many of the new findings reported here. He has read and improved successive drafts of the text and, more than anyone else, has helped me to bring this book into being. Geoffrey Fisher has generously shared his knowledge of Edward Pearce's work and has both contributed new ideas and helped me avoid some erroneous ones. His close reading of the text at a late stage was an act of great kindness. If at some points I have speculated more freely than he would find appropriate, the responsibility is, of course, entirely mine.

From an earlier generation of architectural historians, Geoffrey Beard and Kerry Downes provided benign encouragement. My understanding of the interior decoration of the chapel owes much to Alastair Laing and Tim Newbery, both of whose observations were, for me, revelatory. Adam Bowett, Anthony Geraghty, Craig Hartley, David Scrase and Robert Williams all gave generous help on important points.

It has been a great advantage to be able to study the chapel while a fellow of Pembroke College, not only because of the proximity of the building and its records but also because of the supportive and congenial nature of that community. Jayne Ringrose, the College's archivist, to whose researches on Matthew Wren I am much indebted, has done everything possible to make available such relevant material as the archives contain. Peter Meadows, who looks after the College's architectural collection and has himself contributed to the history of the chapel, has been partner in many productive discussions. Pat Aske has been the most helpful and tolerant of librarians.

A more general debt is that to Michael Davies, with whom I collaborated in mounting an exhibition on the chapel in 1994. That was the beginning of this study, and I have benefited ever since from his interest and encouragement. He commented perceptively on an early version of the text, as did Graham Parry (another Pembroke alumnus).

My particular thanks go to my colleague Ian Fleming, who has patiently and expertly taken countless photographs and seen to their digital manipulation. Beate Alldis designed and composed the book and oversaw its printing: her skill and dedication will be evident. Hester Higton was an expert and vigilant copy-editor and Sally Jeffery has given much helpful advice on production and publishing matters.

An account such as this is usually based on a reasonably large corpus of drawings and other documentation. For Pembroke chapel there is very little. The result is that, when a tentative conclusion is first advanced, it is usually hedged around with the words 'perhaps' or 'possibly'. If, later in the text, these are silently strengthened to 'probably', or the qualification is dropped altogether, that is partly because successive tentative conclusions sometimes reinforce each other, and partly, no doubt, because of wishful thinking on my part. The best I can hope for is that this will be found a helpful starting point for further enquiries.

A V G

Prologue

Matthew Wren, the aged Bishop of Ely, died at his London residence on 24 April 1667. He might have been buried in either of those places, but it was to Cambridge that his body was taken, reaching there on Thursday, 9 May. Four coach loads of mourners accompanied the hearse, with others on horseback. Church bells tolled as the body passed through the town. Wren lay in state for two days in the University Registry, his coffin draped with a gold-embroidered pall, a silver-gilt mitre standing at the head of the coffin, a silver-gilt crozier beside it, four poor scholars keeping watch. Then, in the middle of the afternoon on Saturday, 11 May, there took place one of the grandest funerals that Cambridge had seen.

Although professing a desire 'to avoid that pompe and vanity which is now too much in use,' Matthew Wren had planned his funeral in detail, codicils to his will even specifying the order of the mourners and what they were to wear (Fig. 1).[1] A large and splendid procession accordingly made its way through the town towards Pembroke College, led, as was the custom, by '2 old men in course mourning gownes' carrying black staves (one of them a certain Billops, whom we shall encounter again). Then came twenty-eight poor scholars (seven from each of the colleges – Pembroke, Peterhouse, Jesus and St John's – with which Wren had been associated), followed by the Bishop's servants and chaplains, twenty to thirty in number. Immediately before the coffin walked the Master of Trinity College, Dr John Pearson, and the Master of Pembroke, Dr Robert Mapletoft, along with Francis Sandford, Rouge Dragon Poursuivant, carrying the crozier, and the famous antiquary William Dugdale, Norroy King of Arms, carrying the mitre. It was Dugdale who was stage-managing the whole event in accordance with Wren's wishes. The coffin was 'borne by 6 ordinary persons in course gownes whereof Corn[elius] Austin the joyner was one' – we shall also meet him again. Four prebends of Ely secured the pall. After the coffin came Wren's sons and close relatives, then the Vice-Chancellor of the University, the Heads of Colleges, the Doctors of Divinity in their scarlet robes, the Bachelors of Divinity and finally all the Masters of Arts in their habits and hoods. The Fellows of Pembroke, waiting at the entrance to the College, joined the cortège, which made its way to the chapel – the New Chapel, less than two years old and Matthew Wren's gift to

---

1 A copy of Matthew Wren's will is in PCA, MS Kζ.

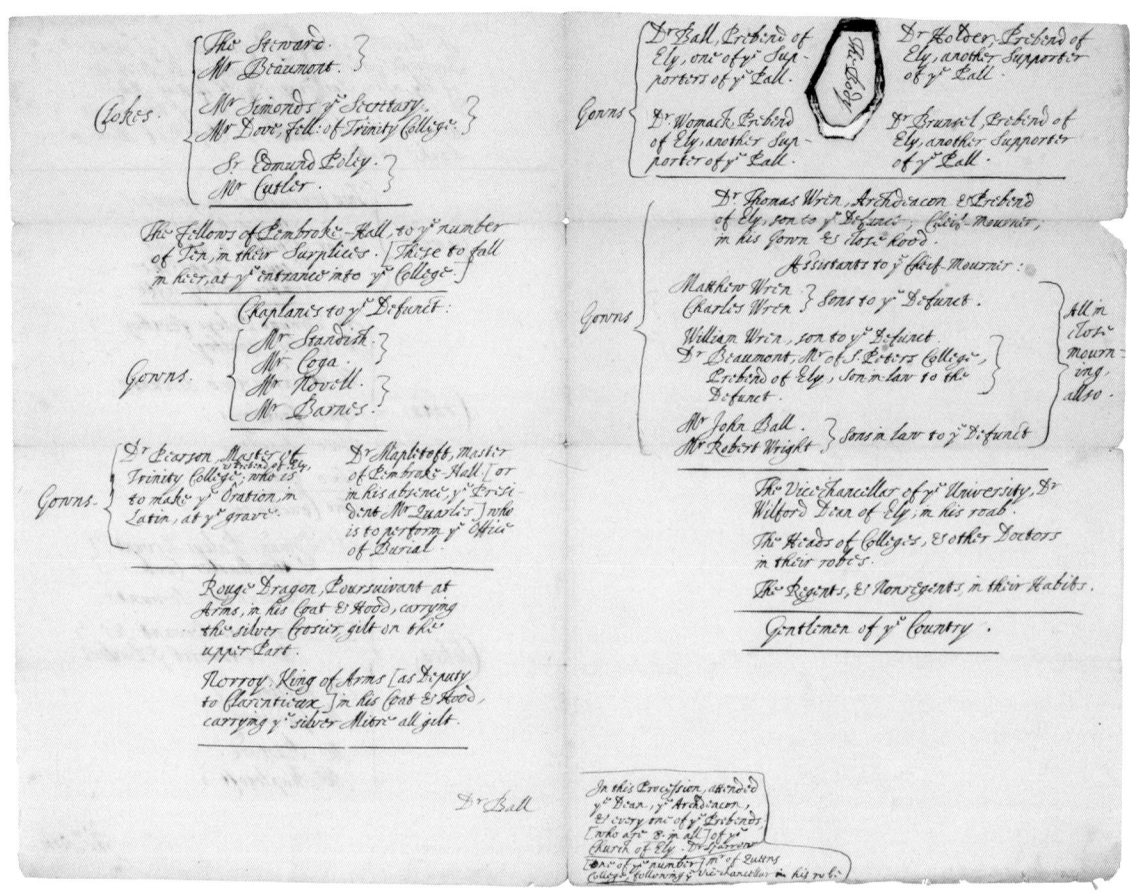

1. Two pages from the order of Matthew Wren's funeral procession, 'The Body' prominent within a coffin-shaped outline at the top. (PCA.)

Pembroke. His nephew, the architect Christopher Wren, was probably among the mourners. The Master of Trinity delivered the Latin funeral oration, exhorting his hearers to look upon the insignia of the Bishop's office, 'brought like trophies back to Athens'. The Master of Pembroke performed the office of burial. Then the Bishop's remains were taken down into the vault below the chapel. As he had planned, his last resting place was the College he had entered as a youth, sixty-five years earlier.[2]

---

2 This account of Matthew Wren's funeral is derived from J E Foster (ed.), 'The diary of Samuel Newton alderman of Cambridge (1662–1717)', *Cambridge Antiquarian Society Octavo Publications*, no. 23 (1890), 18–20, from which the quotations are taken; see also the anonymous account in *PAG*, 5 (1931), 9–12. The mitre and crozier referred to are in the College's collection.

INTRODUCTION

Loggan's engraving of Pembroke College, probably made in 1681–82 (Fig. 2), presents the unusual sight of a Cambridge college with two chapels.[3] The first was probably finished by about 1385, as part of the building campaign that followed the College's foundation in 1347. That chapel was later converted into a library. The other, dating from 1663–65, is the College's present chapel. This book is an attempt to describe its building history: why and how it came into being and the changes it has subsequently undergone.

The starting point must be the donor, Bishop Matthew Wren, uncle of the architect, who met the entire cost of the building. The reasons for his gift, interesting in the history of the times and as an episode in architectural patronage, also bear importantly on the nature of the chapel that was built.

More important than the gift, however, is the fact that Pembroke chapel, begun in 1663 and completed in 1665, is usually taken to be Christopher Wren's first building. (His other early building, the much larger Sheldonian Theatre, Oxford, was begun in 1664 and not finished until 1669; its planning probably also began slightly later than that of Pembroke chapel.)[4] How did it come about that the Savilian Professor of Astronomy in Oxford, aged thirty-one when the building of the chapel began and untutored in architecture, designed the first wholly Classical chapel of any Oxford or Cambridge college? The building would mark the shift in Wren's interests from science to architecture, and it is surprising that there has been no previous attempt to trace its building history.

The main factor that has discouraged investigation is no doubt the dearth of source materials, both in the College's archives and elsewhere: drawings, correspondence, accounts are all few and far between. Indeed, the documentation is so poor that one may reasonably ask what grounds there are for thinking that Wren designed the chapel. Apart from the lack of positive evidence for his involvement, another awkward fact has to be taken into account. The book *Parentalia*, compiled mainly by the architect's son as

3 David Loggan, *Cantabrigia Illustrata* (Cambridge, 1690). Although this was published in 1690, the engraving of Pembroke is dedicated to Nathaniel Coga, Master of the College, described as 'Procancellariatu', and was therefore probably made in 1681–82, when Coga was Vice-Chancellor.
4 Anthony Geraghty, 'Wren's preliminary design for the Sheldonian Theatre', *Architectural History*, 45 (2002), 275–88.

an act of homage to the Wren family,[5] though recording in several places Matthew Wren's gift of the chapel, consistently fails to mention that his nephew designed it. *Parentalia* can hardly be described as well edited, but the absence of a great architect's first commission is unlikely to be due to carelessness. The present study suggests a possible explanation of this disconcerting omission. Wren can justifiably be regarded as the architect of the chapel, but both at the earliest stage of planning – quite probably before Wren was involved – and also at a later stage, someone else, more experienced than Wren in design and craftsmanship, made important contributions. This was Edward Pearce, the sculptor, carver, stone mason and architect. Subsequently, there was to be an important and lengthy association between these men. That this dates from the very beginning of Wren's architectural career is one of the most interesting findings of this study.

The scarcity of documentation about the chapel, while making certainty on all points unattainable, leads one to examine what does survive with perhaps more than usual care. Inevitably, at some points the chapel's building history can be fleshed out only by recourse to circumstantial evidence; sometimes only a series of clues can be offered, individually inconclusive but in sum (it is hoped) persuasive. Certainty on all points is not at present achievable but the main outlines of the story seem to be fairly clear. It can be explained why the chapel was built. The sources of the design and the factors that influenced the eventual shape of the building can be traced. The major craftsmen can be identified fairly confidently. The chronology of the planning and construction of the chapel can be established with reasonable certainty and shows that the building went up rapidly, this haste leading at several points to uncertainties in the design.

Wren and Pearce were not the only architects to work on the chapel. In 1879–81 George Gilbert Scott junior extended it by adding a further bay at the east end to form a new sanctuary: interesting in itself and to be considered in its place. However, for present purposes, almost more important than what he built is the fact that Scott had the chapel accurately surveyed prior to beginning work. These drawings, which survive in the collection of the Royal Institute of British Architects, do not appear to have been previously studied. At numerous points they provide invaluable information about the chapel as originally built.

---

5 Christopher Wren Jr (ed.), *Parentalia or memoirs of the family of the Wrens* (London, 1750, reprinted Farnborough, 1965). Consisting largely of quotations and reprints of documents, *Parentalia* was compiled by the architect's son and published by his grandson, Stephen Wren. It is still a major source of information about both Matthew and Christopher Wren.

INTRODUCTION

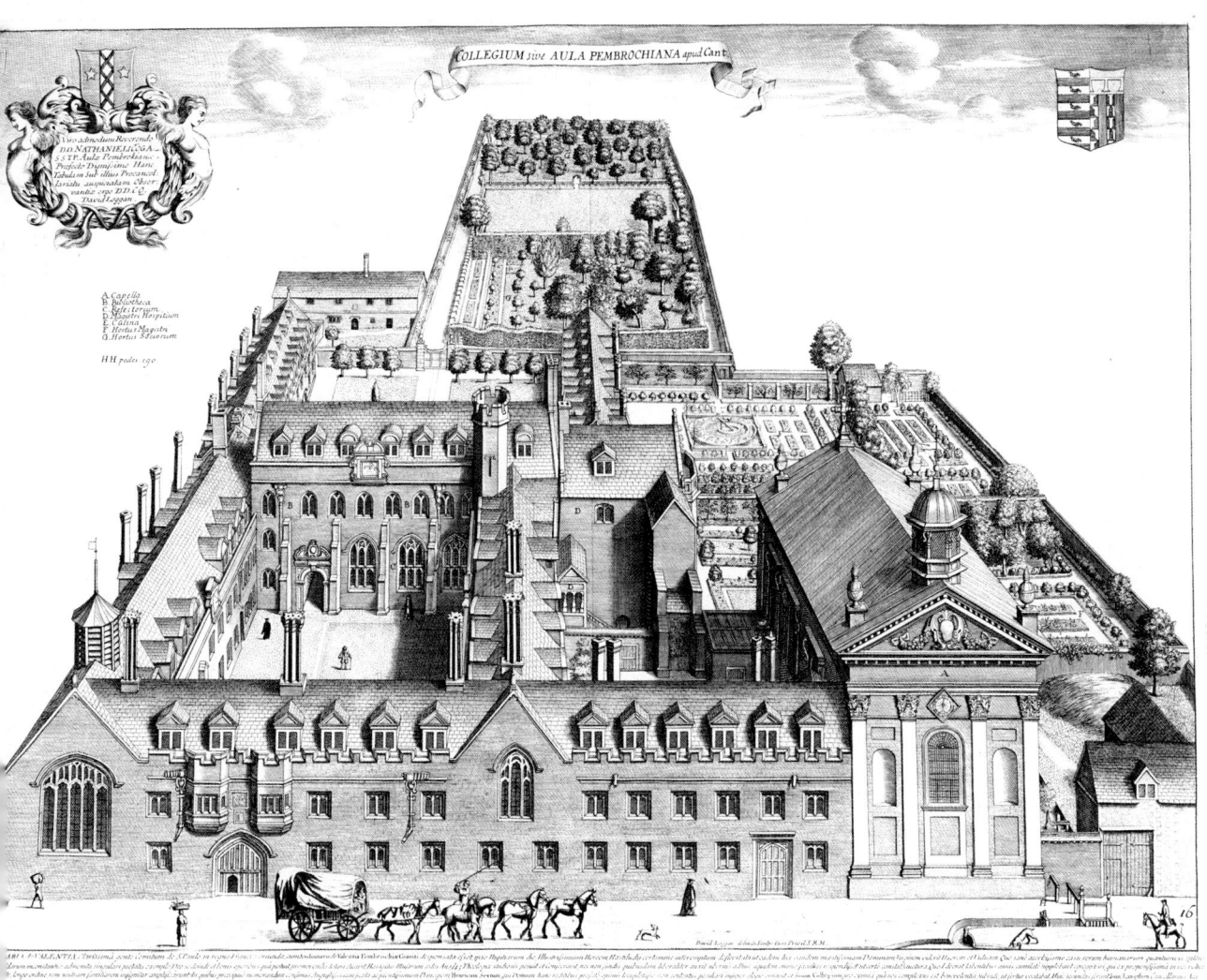

2. Pembroke College, from David Loggan's *Cantabrigia illustrata* (published 1690, the engraving probably made in 1681/2). The medieval Old Court is to the left, with the west window of the old chapel at the far left. The new chapel is on the right. Beyond Old Court are the north and south ranges of Ivy Court, also seventeenth-century.

THE DONOR AND HIS GIFT: MATTHEW WREN

There appears to be no record at Pembroke or elsewhere that specifically documents Matthew Wren's offer of a new chapel or the College's acceptance of it. However, that it was his gift is one of the best attested facts about the chapel, for it is recorded several times in *Parentalia*:

> The first Money he receiv'd after his Restitution he bestow'd on *Pembroke-Hall*, and to the Honour of Almighty God, to whose Service he had wholly devoted himself; for the Ornament of the *University*, which he always affected with a fervent and passionate Love; and in grateful Remembrance of his first Education, which was in that Place receiv'd, and thankfully acknowledg'd, he built that most elegant *Chapel* there, at the Expence of above *five Thousand Pounds*, completely finish'd, and endow'd it with *perpetual Revenues* for Repairs.[6]

Additional information and a slight modification come in another passage:

> He was a very great benefactor to the College in Money and Books; but especially, in erecting at his Charge (it cost him near 4000*l*) that goodly Fabrick the new Chapel; the Altar of which, he furnish'd with his own Chapel Plate; and endowed it with the Royalty of *Hardwick* in this County, to keep it in repair.[7]

The actual cost of the chapel in a general bill given by the college to Matthew Wren on 28 December 1665 was £3658. 1s. 5d.[8] The £5000 mentioned in the first extract probably includes the Hardwick endowment.

Conspicuous in both of these statements is the absence of any reference – where it might surely have been expected – to his nephew having been the architect of the chapel. As we shall see later (p. 20), the tradition that the chapel was designed by Wren was current by 1753. *Parentalia* was published in 1750 and its compiler can scarcely have been unaware of this tradition. The perplexing uncertainty that seems to hang here over Wren's involvement in the design of the chapel is one of the most important issues that will be addressed in this book.

---

6   Christopher Wren Jr, *Parentalia*, 33.
7   Ibid., 45.
8   PCA, Hardwick accounts (MS Mε1), vol. 1.

The gift of the chapel is, however, certain, and its background may be briefly sketched.[9] Matthew Wren (born 23 December 1585) was of modest origins. His father, Francis Wren, owned a shop in Cheapside, in London, and was a mercer, mainly selling the finer kinds of fabric (silk and velvet).[10] Matthew and his brother (another Christopher, father of the architect) must both have been able boys: they finished their schooling at Merchant Taylors' School and both went on to university, Matthew being admitted as an undergraduate at Pembroke College in June 1601. There he was the protégé of Lancelot Andrewes, Master of the College, later Bishop of Ely and of Winchester, and probably the most important influence on Wren's life.

Reserved, subtle, learned, renowned as teacher and preacher and revered for his piety and integrity, Andrewes was the greatest of the many churchmen produced by Pembroke in the sixteenth century. As Geoffrey Webb wrote,

> that great man had not only the gift of divining merit in his followers, but of lending to his chosen something of his own extraordinary distinction of outlook . . . it was men like Andrewes who themselves constituted the splendour of the Stuart court, the loveliness of the Church of England and the greatness of her learned tradition.[11]

It would have been Andrewes' example that led to Matthew Wren's dedicated life of religious scholarship, his high-Anglican orientation and his devotion to the liturgy and ceremonies of the church; it was through Andrewes' influence that he gained entry to the Stuart court. In time he would become Andrewes' most important follower.

Matthew Wren became a fellow of Pembroke in 1605 and by 1621 had risen to be both Bursar and President (that is, Vice-Master). His strengths were energy, determination, a capacity for tireless application and a passion for order. An austere man – 'His habits throughout life were those of a hardy scholar, up at five and seldom in bed till eleven' – he was a disciplinarian, intolerant of laziness or insubordination. His portrait (Fig. 3) shows him with the outmoded ruff that he habitually wore, perhaps indicative of his conservatism. He was devoted to Pembroke and is remembered there, apart from his gift of the chapel, for his painstaking study of the College's history and his copying and arrangement of ancient documents.

Wren's activities in Pembroke ran in parallel with the intertwined strands of his career in the church (ordained deacon and priest in 1611, he became

---

9 There is no modern biography of Matthew Wren. The fullest treatment is in Peter King, 'Matthew Wren, Bishop of Hereford, Norwich and Ely, 1585–1667' (unpublished PhD thesis, University of Bristol, 1969). Hugh Trevor-Roper, 'Little Pope Regulus: Matthew Wren, Bishop of Norwich and Ely', in *From counter-reformation to Glorious Revolution* (London, 1992), 151–71, provides a shorter assessment.
10 There appears to be no foundation for the claims that he was a Freeman of the City and member of the Mercers' Company.
11 Geoffrey Webb, *Wren* (London, 1937), 12.

3. Matthew Wren. Artist and provenance unknown; oil on canvas. The engraving of Wren in *Parentalia* by Gerard Van der Gucht, similar to this portrait but reversed, is described as 'from an original Picture of him, before his Advancement to the Prelacy, being about thirty Years of Age'. This painting, at Pembroke College, is probably that original picture.

chaplain to Andrewes in 1615) and his association with the court. In time he would become a 'courtier bishop'. When, in 1623, Prince Charles went to Madrid in his farcical and abortive attempt to win the hand of the Infanta Isabella, Wren accompanied him as one of his two chaplains.[12]

The visit to Spain, lasting six months, was the beginning of a close relationship between Charles and Wren. Perhaps the journey had other consequences. Apart from seeking a wife, another preoccupation of Charles (and of the Duke of Buckingham, also of the party) was the acquisition of paintings. In this they were aided by Sir Balthazar Gerbier, courtier, man of parts and architectural adviser to Buckingham and, in time, to Archbishop

---

12 Glyn Redworth, *The Prince and the Infanta* (New Haven and London, 2003).

Laud. Contact with two ardent collectors may have aroused Wren's interest in aesthetic matters generally, and his meeting with Gerbier might have directed his thoughts towards architecture: first at Peterhouse, Cambridge, later at Pembroke. Gerbier was to write two minor architectural works: *A brief discourse concerning the three chief principles of magnificent building* (1662) and *Counsel and advise to all builders* (1663), which would appear just as planning of Pembroke chapel began. More important than this contact with Gerbier, however, is that, through his association with the court, Matthew Wren would almost certainly have come into contact with Inigo Jones, who was providing designs for masques and other court entertainments from about 1605 to 1640. Wren would no doubt have seen Jones's major London building projects take shape: the Banqueting House of 1619–22, or the later remodelling of the exterior of St Paul's of 1633–42.

Wren remained a fellow of Pembroke until 1624, when he resigned on receiving the royal living of Bingham, Nottinghamshire. He was there only briefly for, when Charles became king, an act of royal preferment returned Wren to Cambridge in 1625 as Master of Peterhouse. Here he displayed the same zeal in such tasks as the ordering of historical documents and the cataloguing of the library as he had at Pembroke. He is chiefly remembered at Peterhouse, however, for having initiated the building of the college chapel, previously lacking. Wren raised money for this project[13] and was certainly responsible for the Laudian arrangement of the interior.[14] The work of an unknown architect, the chapel is confused in style, with leanings towards the Renaissance yet largely using a simplified Perpendicular style; Pevsner describes it as architecturally 'the most remarkable building of its date in Cambridge'.[15] Begun in 1628 and consecrated in 1633, it was not completed until about 1665, the year in which Pembroke chapel was consecrated; a possible connection between the two buildings is noted later (p. 131, n.).

Matthew Wren's growing intimacy with the court during this time and his devotion to the king are shown by his appointments as Dean of the Chapel Royal, Dean of Windsor and registrar to the Order of the Garter. His attendance on Charles for his Scottish coronation must surely also indicate considerable closeness to the king. Public recognition and reward came, perhaps belatedly, in 1634 with his first appointment as bishop.

The initial phase of Wren's episcopal career lasted only seven years, when he was successively bishop of Hereford, Norwich and Ely. He became one of the most important bishops of his time, 'the efficient and trusted ally' of

---

13 Jayne Ringrose, 'Matthew Wren makes his will', *PAG*, 67 (1993), 21–26. Wren refers in his will to the Peterhouse chapel, 'which I did obteine to be built'.
14 Graham Parry, *Glory, Laud and honour: the arts of the Anglican counter-reformation* (Woodbridge, 2008), 7–9.
15 Nikolaus Pevsner, *Cambridgeshire* (Harmondsworth, 1970), 132.

Archbishop Laud. Writing of Wren's career as a bishop, Phillimore perhaps judged him fairly:

> That [Matthew] Wren was a great upholder of discipline and authority, a man of fiery energetic temper, decided opinions, and an unyielding, perhaps severe disposition, is certainly true; but it is also true that he practised ... an even-handed justice, laying his hand on rich and poor alike, and would not turn aside for any suggestion of policy or expediency.[16]

Wren's tireless efforts to enforce high-Anglican practices – particularly in the vast diocese of Norwich with its substantial Puritan faction – led inevitably to resentment, hostility, pamphlet attacks and unrest. His translation from Norwich to Ely in 1638 was at least in part an attempt to deflect this opposition. It was also a reward, for Ely, a much grander see than Norwich, was a palatinate, in which the bishop controlled valuable rights. Wren's skill and energy in handling these resources to build up his own fortune and to bestow on his relatives valuable livings and other offices is relevant to his later gift of the new Pembroke chapel. His reputation in the country at large was, however, scarcely affected by the move to Ely, and it was in the national setting of the conflict between king and parliament and between Puritans and the Laudian bishops that Wren came under sustained attack. Articles of impeachment against him were drawn up in 1641. Never brought to trial, he was imprisoned in the Tower of London from August 1642 to March 1660. The execution of Laud in 1645 and of Charles I in 1649 would have been for him catastrophic events in the life of church and nation.

The last of Matthew Wren's fourteen children was conceived while he was in the Tower, so the conditions of his captivity were presumably by no means excessively harsh. He was able to study and write and no doubt reflect on the revision of the Book of Common Prayer, a task he had long contemplated and for which he was supremely qualified. He was also, surprisingly, able to intervene in the affairs of his diocese, at least until 1645. At some point during his captivity Wren conceived the idea of making a thank-offering, should he ever be released from the Tower. In his will he writes:

> I had bound myselfe by a secret promise in my prison unto the Almighty That if ever it should please him to restore my auncient estate unto me, I should retourne unto him by some holy and pious employment, that summe and more wch by way of his gracious providence was unexpectedly conveyed unto me during my Eighteen yeares captivity in the Tower of London...[17]

16 Lucy Phillimore, *Sir Christopher Wren, his family and times* (London, 1881), 26.
17 The means by which Wren was able to receive money while imprisoned are unclear. After he was reinstated as Bishop of Ely he would once more have had access to the revenues of the diocese. At the time of his death in 1667 he was a wealthy man, able to provide bequests of £2500 and dowries of £2000 for each of his four surviving daughters (Ringrose, 'Matthew Wren makes his will', 22; King, *Matthew Wren*, 18).

This 'holy and pious employment' was to be the building of the new Pembroke chapel.

Why did he choose this for his thank-offering? Wren almost certainly had multiple intentions. However, the creation of a personal memorial seems not to have been one of them, for within the building there is nothing to inform us of his gift: no inscription, no sign of Wren's episcopal arms (except in the stall cushions he bequeathed), no bishop's mitre, no wrens worked into the carvings in allusion to his name; there must have been other reasons.[18]

That Wren should have wished to make a gift of some sort to Pembroke is unsurprising: twenty-three years in the College at the most formative period of his life would be sufficient explanation. However, more specific motives for the benefaction and its particular form may reasonably be sought.

A reason initially suggesting itself is that the old chapel was perhaps dilapidated. Pembroke had been among the first Cambridge colleges to introduce Laudian arrangements within its chapel. By the early 1630s there were a choir and organ, communion rails, candlesticks, an altar cloth and other hangings; in 1628 the whitewash had been removed from the walls, presumably to reveal medieval paintings.[19] Such trappings made it an inevitable target for the Puritans. In 1643 William Dowsing, commissioned to implement in eastern England a Parliamentary Ordinance requiring 'that all Monuments of Superstition and Idolatry should be removed and abolished', began work on the Cambridge colleges and city churches. His *Journal* records: 'At Pembroke-Hall, 1643, December 26. In the presence of Fellowes Mr. Weeden, Mr. Mapthorpe, and Mr Sterne, and Mr. Quarles, and Mr. Felton, we broak 10 cherubims. We broak and pulled down 80 superstitious pictures'.[20]

The eighty pictures were perhaps partly in the windows (glazed in the mid-fifteenth century with the four Doctors of the Church and various saints),[21] partly on the walls. The chapel would no doubt have looked forlorn after the attentions of Dowsing's men. However, there is nothing to suggest that it suffered structural damage. In Loggan's engraving (Fig. 2) the old chapel appears intact and, as far as is known, it continued in use until the new chapel was consecrated in 1665. It is thus improbable that a new chapel was offered because the old one was in ruins. Nor can it have seemed too small, for the

---

18 The letter 'W' occurs on the rainwater heads. However, these were renewed by Scott, who provided a design for them and perhaps introduced the 'W'. (Letter from Rattee & Kett [builders] to Scott, 7 August 1880: 'Forming lead gutters, with 4 stacks of downpipes and ornamental heads to design would probably be about £80' (RIBA Collection, SC/CA/PC/246).

19 Aubrey Attwater, *Pembroke College Cambridge: a short history* (Cambridge, 1936), 68.

20 Trevor Cooper (ed.), *The journal of William Dowsing: iconoclasm in East Anglia during the English Civil War* (Woodbridge, 2001), 161–2.

21 Graham Chainey, 'The lost stained glass of Cambridge', *Proceedings of the Cambridge Antiquarian Society*, 79 (1990), 70–81.

internal area of the new chapel usable for worship – that is, excluding its ante-chapel – was to be only about six per cent greater than that of the old one.

Wren's intentions become clearer when we find that from the outset he wished the new chapel to be his burial place. In his will he writes:

> Now of this New Chappell haveing purposely caused the East end to be soe raysed, as that under the holy table there is a Vault strongly inclosed, My Will is that (If God soe please) it shalbe for my owne Sepulture, and for the interring of the succeeding Masters of the said College if they shall have a minde thereto...[22]

In making this provision he was departing from the custom that bishops of Ely were buried in the cathedral. Wren probably foresaw that, unpopular in Ely, he would not be interred there and would, in fact, not be commemorated in the cathedral at all.[23] His wish to secure a burial place commensurate with his status is understandable. However, important as was this aim, it can hardly have been the sole reason for his gift: the creation of an entirely new college chapel as a personal mausoleum seems disproportionate.

To suggest other reasons is to venture onto less secure ground. However, there were certainly other thoughts in Wren's mind at about this time, apparent as he composed his lengthy will. Of this, Jayne Ringrose writes, 'It shows a man conscious of his own dignity, and of that of the Church of England, the Monarchy and the University, deliberately seeking to assert the worth of these institutions, which had nearly been destroyed and himself with them during the Rebellion.'[24]

As Kerry Downes has suggested, Wren probably intended the new chapel as a symbolic affirmation of 'Restoration', signalling a return to normality after years of disruption and anarchy.[25] Seventy-four years old at the time of his release, Matthew Wren was himself too old and out of touch to play any significant part in the politics of the time: he seems to have met Charles II only once, disapproved of his profligate life and made no attempt to be readmitted to court favour. Nevertheless, the restoration of the monarchy would have been of paramount importance to him. Likewise, in the Church, the bishops were back in office and the Anglican doctrines and Laudian practices that Wren had tirelessly promoted were reaffirmed. At a personal level, Wren's release from captivity and reinstatement as Bishop of Ely had restored his freedom and dignity, marked by the costly ceremony celebrating his return to Ely.[26] If the new chapel was to symbolise this return to an authentic state

---

22 Wren goes on to suggest that benefactors of over one hundred pounds and his own (male) descendants might also be interred there.
23 Information from Peter Meadows.
24 Ringrose, 'Matthew Wren makes his will', 21. The will runs to over 12,000 words.
25 Kerry Downes, *The architecture of Wren*, 2nd edn (Reading, 1988), 32.
26 King, *Matthew Wren*, 330.

of affairs, it would need to be striking in design and outwardly impressive: aims that could be achieved by making it Cambridge's 'earliest purely Classical building',[27] 'the first college chapel in [Oxford or Cambridge] to be completely void of Gothic features'[28] and prominently located.[29]

Important as this affirmation of Restoration no doubt was, there was perhaps yet another reason for his gift of the chapel. As bishop of Ely, Wren had from the outset worked to bring Cambridge University increasingly within the Church's orbit. As we have seen, he had himself been Master of Peterhouse and was Vice-Chancellor of the University in 1628–29. As bishop he had considerable power in Cambridge: able to appoint the Master of Jesus College and, as Visitor of Peterhouse and St John's College, acting as the ultimate court of appeal in disputed mastership elections. He had a barge to convey him between Ely and Cambridge. Perhaps the new Pembroke chapel was to signify his influence in the University.

Gratitude to Pembroke, a personal mausoleum, a symbol of Restoration and an affirmation of the bishop's power in Cambridge: collectively, the possible reasons are more than enough to explain Matthew Wren's gift of the new chapel.

---

27 Pevsner, *Cambridgeshire*, 27.
28 John Summerson, *Architecture in Britain 1530–1830*. 9th edn (New Haven and London, 1993), 182.
29 This was not the first use of Classical design, harking back to more propitious times, to symbolise Restoration. It was used notably in the design of the triumphal arches erected in the City for Charles II's coronation procession in April 1661 (see p. 38). For a discussion of the various seventeenth-century connotations of 'Restoration' and their expression in the arts, see Graham Parry, *The seventeenth century: the intellectual and cultural context of English literature, 1603–1700* (London, 1989).

THE SEVENTEENTH-CENTURY CHAPEL

THE PRESENT BUILDING

It may be useful to begin with a brief description of the chapel as it now is, and of the alterations it has undergone since its completion in 1665.[30] The chapel is a simple building, rectangular in plan (Fig. 4). The only major alteration to its original state has been the addition, in the nineteenth century, of a new bay at the east end, designed by George Gilbert Scott junior.

Beginning with the exterior, it is on the west front, facing onto the street and dressed wholly with stone, that, in keeping with the building's presumed symbolic intention, the Classical style is most fully deployed and the richest decoration is found (Fig. 19). This all appears to be essentially unaltered. A hexagonal cupola rises above this end; like the flaming urns on the corners of the chapel (which also occur at the east end), it formed part of the original design (Fig. 2).

The side elevations (Fig. 5) are identical, except that there are three windows on the north side, but four on the south, since on the latter the chapel does not abut any other building. These elevations now mostly display brickwork, apart from the stone plinth, the cornice and the dressings around the windows and around the panels below them. All this belongs to the original building, except that, when the chapel, was built the bricks were covered with stucco, which Scott removed. The last (east) bay, Scott's work, is faced wholly

---

30 The fullest description of the chapel is in RCHM *Cambridge,* part 2, 148 and 153–4.

4. Scott's survey plan of the original chapel, showing it essentially as built. The east end is at the top. The chapel is entered via the ante-chapel, from the cloister, two piers of the arcade of which are shown. The square drawn between the first pier and the chapel is the outline of one of the two structures that originally gave access to the rooms above the cloister. In the screen between chapel and ante-chapel, the paired semicircular recesses on each side are the stalls for the Master and President and other senior fellows or visitors. Coupled timber columns frame the entrance into the chapel from the ante-chapel. The stalls fill the body of the chapel. A single step, then two steps, bring one to the communion rails, which stretch the full width of the building. Beyond this, the altar is sited below the east window. Almost everything here survives, except for the ends of the communion rails. Scott moved the door into the chapel eastwards (indicated here), to allow rooms to be built along the west side of the cloister. Note the slight asymmetry of the west end of the ante-chapel. (RIBA Library Collections, SCGGJ[13]85.)

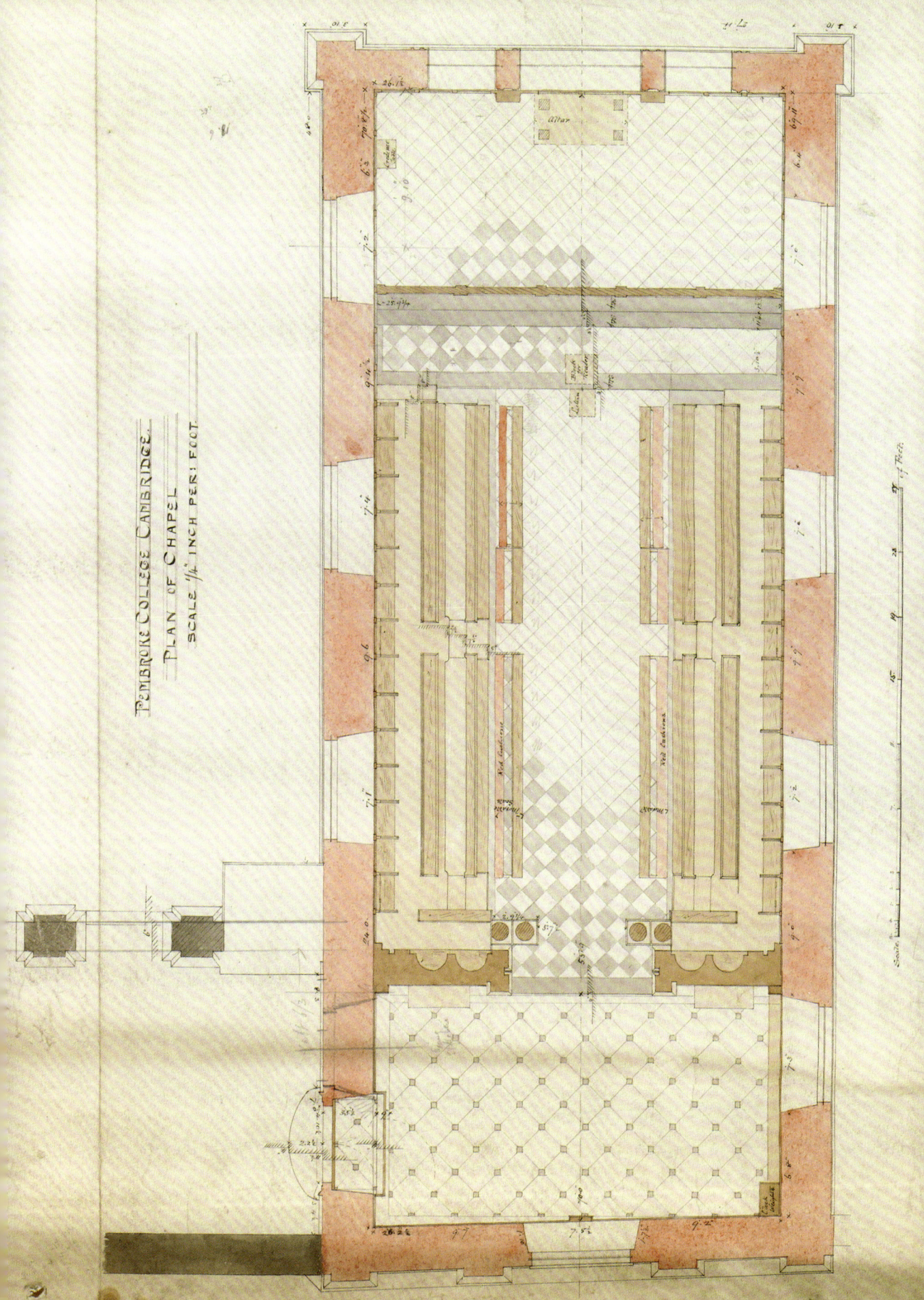

THE SEVENTEENTH-CENTURY CHAPEL

5. The chapel, from the north. Scott's ashlared east bay (1880) is to the left, the south end of the cloister to the right. The position of the present entrance to the vault is visible at ground level, below the left-hand jamb of the left-hand window. (Edward Leigh, c.1974)

with stone. The pedimented niches in the sides of this bay are of his design and were not represented in the original building. The chapel is entered at the west end of the north side, from the adjoining cloister (which is contemporary with the chapel). Alterations made to the cloister by Scott necessitated moving the entrance a few feet east but it is still within the cloister.

The east elevation, dominated by its three-light Serliana or Venetian window (Fig. 22), is of stone. This is original (that is, seventeenth-century) work: when Scott's new bay was created, the original east wall of the chapel was taken down and its external stonework (if not its internal brickwork) reassembled to form the east wall of the new sanctuary. The corner pilasters at this end are probably also those of the original building but the pilasters on the sides of the chapel, at the junctions of the original sides with those of Scott's extension, though identical in style to those on the corners, must be part of Scott's work.

Entering the chapel, one finds oneself in a panelled ante-chapel extending the full width of the building, with the organ loft above. The chapel itself was originally a single space, the east end being set apart from the body of the chapel (with its stalls) only by its raised floor level, by the communion rails and by differences in the style of the decorative wood-carving. Looking westwards now from the east end (Fig. 39) most of what one sees – the stalls and panelling, the ornate plaster ceiling, the plaster decorations above the windows and the black-and-white marble floor – is original work of the seventeenth century, little changed.

The major change internally is the radical reshaping of the east end brought about by Scott. His new bay allowed the formation of a structurally distinct sanctuary, set apart by a grand arch supported on columns and pilasters, which now forms the dominant feature of the interior (Fig. 80). The communion rails, in reduced form, were shifted eastwards and some additional steps were introduced. The panelling and reredos of the new sanctuary is largely that of the original east end, though the reredos underwent some significant alterations. The decorative carving on the side walls of the original east end of the chapel was also moved into the new sanctuary, the gaps thus left being filled by new carving in the same style as that above the stalls. Below the original east end of the chapel is the vault in which Matthew Wren and others are interred.

The external dimensions of the chapel, including the ante-chapel and Scott's new bay, are approximately 95 feet by 33 feet (29 metres by 10 metres).

PERSONALIA

It will be argued here that, although Christopher Wren was indeed chiefly responsible for the eventual overall design of Pembroke chapel and may therefore reasonably be regarded as 'the architect' of the building, he was not first in the field or the only contributor to the design: the earliest and almost the only drawing we have for the chapel exterior is not by Wren. There is also evidence of another hand in the design of the interior. In both cases the other person involved appears to have been Edward Pearce. In this section, therefore, a brief account of both men must be given.

Christopher Wren (1632–1723)

In most accounts of Wren's work it is accepted that Pembroke chapel was his first building. No one but Wren has hitherto been suggested as the architect. However, as we have noted, there is no record of his being commissioned to design the chapel and *Parentalia* fails to list it among his buildings. A contemporary report of the consecration of the chapel also fails to mention the architect.[31] The case for Wren clearly needs examination.

The traditional belief (as it may be called) that Wren designed the chapel was current by 1753 at the latest, when it appears in the first guidebook to Cambridge to be published after the chapel was built.[32] A persuasive argument in support of this belief is the fact that, within about a year of the consecration of Pembroke chapel, Wren was commissioned by another high-Anglican cleric, William Sancroft, to design a chapel for Emmanuel College, Cambridge.[33] The similarities between the two buildings suggest rather strongly that Pembroke chapel was the forerunner of that at Emmanuel. Less convincing but perhaps relevant is the fact that Wren was associated with Pembroke not only through his uncle but by being the brother-in-law of William Holder, who had been an undergraduate and briefly fellow (1640–42) of the College. Holder, married to Wren's sister Susan,[34] was an able mathematician and natural

---

31 *The Intelligencer*, Monday 2 October 1665 (no. 80), 945; see Willis and Clark, vol. 1, 621.
32 Edmund Carter, *The history of the University of Cambridge: from its original, to the year 1753* (London, 1753), 77: 'The building was executed according to a Plan designed by the great Architect Sir Christopher Wren'.
33 Frank Stubbings, *Emmanuel College chapel, 1677–1977* (Emmanuel College, Cambridge, 1977).
34 There is a memorial to William and Susan Holder in the crypt of St Paul's cathedral, close to that of Wren.

philosopher and an early member of the Royal Society. During the civil war, when the Wren family had taken refuge at Holder's rectory at Bletchingdon, near Oxford, Holder was an influential figure in the young Wren's education and taught him mathematics. All this is, of course, far from decisive. Howard Colvin, in the 1995 edition of his *Biographical dictionary of British architects*, with understandable hesitancy, could only designate the chapel as 'attributed' in his list of Wren's works.[35]

This situation was to a degree improved in 1994 by the discovery, in the Pembroke archives, of a document containing jottings about procuring the marble flooring of the chapel. In his account of this document, Peter Meadows presents reasons for thinking that it is in Wren's hand.[36] This important finding will be discussed later (p. 106–8); it does not in itself prove Wren's role as architect or explain why he is not credited with the design of the chapel in *Parenatalia*. Some new evidence that links him rather more convincingly to the design of the chapel has emerged in the course of this study and will be presented in its place (p. 43–4). It has also been found that, with few exceptions, the same group of craftsmen worked on the Pembroke and Emmanuel chapels (see p. 115). Finally, the exterior of Pembroke chapel displays some of what would become characteristic stylistic features of Wren's architecture. In sum, this seems to justify the conclusion that he had, at the very least, a major role in the design of the chapel.

At the time of the commission to design the chapel Wren was Professor of Astronomy at Oxford. The circumstances that enabled him to switch into architecture have been abundantly discussed elsewhere,[37] but I will summarise here. In the mid-seventeenth century, architecture and science were not seen as distinct areas of knowledge. At that time the architectural profession scarcely existed in England. Even large country houses commonly came into being through the collaboration of the owner – consulting the treatises of Palladio, Serlio and others – with a mason or bricklayer who understood the practicalities of building. The early members of the Royal Society, who frequently discussed architecture, treated it not as a distinct branch of knowledge and practice but as one of the mathematical sciences, together with such cognate subjects as astronomy, surveying, cartography, navigation, fortifications, engines, machines and the measurement of quantities of all kinds. They interested themselves, too, in the structure of buildings and the

---

35 In the most recent edition (Howard Colvin, *A biographical dictionary of British architects, 1600–1840*. 4th edn (New Haven and London, 2008), 1157), Colvin lists the chapel as Wren's, without qualification.

36 P M Meadows, 'Sir Christopher Wren and Pembroke chapel', *Georgian Group Journal*, 4 (1994), 55–7; reprinted in *PAG*, 68 (1994), 25–9.

37 Geoffrey Webb, *Wren* (London, 1937); John Summerson, Sir Christopher Wren (London, 1953); John Summerson, 'Christopher Wren: why architecture?', in *The unromantic castle and other essays* (London, 1990); J A Bennett, *The mathematical science of Christopher Wren* (Cambridge, 1982); Lisa Jardine, *On a grander scale* (London, 2002).

properties of building materials. All this was not wholly disinterested, for the embryonic Society was anxious to show its relevance to society at large. From the 1650s, Wren had taken part in these discussions of building matters, as did John Evelyn and Robert Hooke, who both became seriously involved in architecture. At least four other members of the Society, including John Aubrey and John Wallis, applied themselves less assiduously.[38] Important as they were, the Royal Society's interests in architecture were obviously of a somewhat utilitarian nature. Wren would have needed something more in order to design a Classical building, which may help to explain why he needed assistance at the outset of his career.

Wren differed from his Royal Society contemporaries in that, while he never lost his interest in science and mathematics, architecture became his profession. He brought to it, apart from a formidable intellect and an analytical mind, wide-ranging interests in different areas of science, from astronomy to biology. He also had practical abilities that, from his youth, saw him making models to demonstrate visually the workings of the natural world, from the movements of the planets to the functions of the human muscular system: he was able to make the transition from an abstract idea to something that worked in three-dimensions – a precious talent for an architect. His skill as a draughtsman was shown by the drawings he made to illustrate Thomas Willis's anatomical study of the brain, *Cerebri Anatome* (1664), as well as by the multitude of architectural drawings that were to follow.

What Wren might have achieved had he remained a scientist can only be conjectured. John Summerson (never Wren's strongest advocate) suggested that, for all his abilities and the wide range of his interests, 'there is really nothing to which one can point as a crowning achievement in Wren's career as a scientist'.[39] Perhaps architecture was inevitable. Before he received his first two commissions – Pembroke chapel and the Sheldonian Theatre in Oxford, both probably early in 1663 – the king had asked him to advise on the harbour and fortification of Tangier (which he declined to do), and he had been brought into discussions of the repair of old St Paul's cathedral. If he still remained uncertain about the direction his career should take, the Great Fire provided, in Summerson's phrase, 'the pressure of opportunity'.[40]

A model of the Sheldonian Theatre at Oxford, including the novel roof trusses that Wren devised to span the flat ceiling of seventy feet breadth, was exhibited at the Royal Society on 29 April 1663.[41] This was a month before building work began on Pembroke chapel. The foundation stone of the Sheldonian was laid on 26 July 1664 and the building was not completed until 1669, four years after the chapel. Unsurprisingly, both appear to be the work of a gifted amateur.

38   Bennett, *Mathematical science*, 87–89.
39   Summerson, 'Christopher Wren: why architecture?', 66.
40   Ibid, 65.
41   Thomas Birch, *The history of the Royal Society of London* (London, 1756), vol. 1, 230.

Until Pembroke chapel was built there was no convincingly Classical building in Cambridge. Where Classical features were employed, as for example in the Fellows' Building at Christ's College, they were not integrated into a fully worked-out and understood Classical design. The novelty of Pembroke chapel as the first wholly Classical college chapel in Cambridge or Oxford, was surely important for Matthew Wren's symbolic aims in donating it. Elsewhere in England, of course, and in London particularly, there were religious buildings in which the Classical style had been used with complete assurance. Forty years earlier Inigo Jones had designed the Queen's Chapel at St James's Palace and followed it with another chapel at Somerset House and with St Paul's church, Covent Garden: learnedly Classical buildings that (like Jones's Banqueting House) Christopher Wren presumably knew, but at the time of his earliest commissions did not fully appreciate. Writing of the later elevation of Wren over John Webb and Hugh May to be Surveyor-General of the Works, Geoffrey Webb suggested that, 'To a man like Webb, brought up strictly as an architect under Inigo Jones, Wren's extant works in 1669 must have seemed very barbarous and uninstructed.'[42] Summerson's assessment of Pembroke chapel was equally cool:

> The ultimate appraisal of the building must be this: it is constructed with a great deal of thought and expressed in sound Latin [i.e. correct Classical detail]; but in conception it is unimaginative . . . 'Unimaginative' is perhaps too vague. 'Unpoetical' is more exact since it implies the absence of that deft, intuitive, co-ordination of thought and imagination which is exactly what is missing in Pembroke Chapel.[43]

Earlier, Belcher and Macartney had decided that, 'The whole work must be regarded as a youthful composition, faulty, but showing promise of better things', adding that the chapel 'appears to have been somewhat hurriedly executed, for there is a want of finish not found in Wren's later work'.[44] It need hardly be added that, notwithstanding these strictures, it remains of interest to explore how this first building associated with Wren's name came into being.

---

42 Webb, *Wren*, 61–2.
43 John Summerson, 'The mind of Wren', in *Heavenly mansions and other essays on architecture* (London, 1949), 63–4. The essay reprinted here was first published in 1937 with the title 'The tyranny of intellect'. Anthony Geraghty, in his paper 'The "dissociation of sensibility" and the "Tyranny of intellect": T. S. Eliot, John Summerson and Christopher Wren', in Frank Salmon (ed.), *The persistence of the classical* (London, 2009), relates Summerson's censure of Wren (for failing to co-ordinate thought and imagination in his architecture) to T S Eliot's contemporary detection of a comparable 'dissociation of sensibility' in English poetry after Donne.
44 J Belcher and J Macartney, *Later Renaissance architecture in England* (London, 1901), vol. 2, 92.

Edward Pearce (*c*.1635–1695)

Edward Pearce has not previously been connected with Pembroke chapel. However, he was certainly involved with Emmanuel College chapel and was later to work on many other buildings with Wren. His participation at Pembroke, for which evidence will be adduced, is therefore not altogether surprising.

Pearce (also frequently spelled 'Pierce') was born in about 1635 and so was of an age with Wren; he died in 1695. Much of his life is still obscure.[45] He was a man of remarkable talents, the diversity and scale of whose work becomes increasingly apparent. The first substantial article about him, by Rachael Poole in 1923, was entitled, 'Edward Pierce, the Sculptor' and ends, 'When all is said of his other work, it is for the great qualities of his portrait-busts that Pierce deserves to be known and admired'.[46] Since then it is his work as a carver in wood and stone, and as designer, draughtsman, architect and mason that has attracted more attention.

Pearce came of an artistic family. His father (also Edward) was a respected decorative painter and a versatile craftsman, who seems to have been employed at one time as an assistant by van Dyck. For many years he was associated with Inigo Jones who, as Royal Surveyor, employed him in decorative work for the royal apartments and in devising scenery for the masques put on at the Stuart court. He also worked with Jones in decorating Wilton House. As we shall see, he was knowledgeable about decorative design. Two of the elder Pearce's brothers appear to have been painters; and, while Edward is by far the best known and most important of his sons, two others were seemingly painters.[47]

Indicative of the artistic leanings of the family is the fact that both Edward Pearces had their portraits painted by leading artists of the day: the father by William Dobson,[48] the son by the equally competent Isaac Fuller. The portrait of the younger Pearce is valuable for what it shows of the man. It exists in two versions, of which the one at Sudeley Castle, Gloucestershire[49] appears to be a study for the other, now at the Yale Centre for British Art (Fig. 6). With his commanding pose, flowing gown and unsmiling, questioning gaze, he is

---

[45] For summaries of Pearce's life and work see Colvin, *Biographical dictionary*; Katharine Eustace, 'Pearce, Edward', *Oxford dictionary of national biography* (Oxford, 2004); Rupert Gunnis, *Dictionary of British sculptors 1660–1851* (London, 1968; revised edn forthcoming); John Physick, 'Edward Pearce (ii)', in Jane Turner (ed.), *The dictionary of art* (New York and London, 1996), vol. 24, 753–4.

[46] Rachel Poole, 'Edward Pierce, the sculptor', *Walpole Society*, 11 (1922–3), 33–45. Poole states that 'Pierce, as though on purpose, signed his portrait busts Pierce – while as an architect or architectural carver his name always appears as Pearce'.

[47] S J Turner, 'Edward Pierce (i)', in Jane Turner, *Dictionary of art*, vol. 24, 752–3.

[48] The portrait, which seems not to have survived, is referred to by Vertue: Horace Walpole (ed.), *Anecdotes of painting in England . . . collected by the late Mr George Vertue* (Twickenham, 1762–71) vol. 2, 315.

[49] Reproduced in Geoffrey Beard and Cherry A Knott, 'Edward Pearce's work at Sudbury', *Apollo*, 151 (April 2000), 43–8.

6. Edward Pearce, by Isaac Fuller (1606–72); oil on canvas. (Yale Center for British Art.)

far from presenting himself as a mere craftsman: this is a self-confident man who wishes to be seen as an artist. His left hand rests on a copy of a famous antique bust from the Farnese Collection – usually identified as *Aratus*[50] – a replica that he probably owned, for Pearce was a noted collector. His right hand gestures towards something at the bottom right of the painting. Sketchily painted, it is difficult to make out what this is: possibly in part a flower-like decoration, as if this might be a piece of carving, or perhaps something that might be a pair of compasses or a quill pen. Perhaps Pearce is drawing attention to his skill as carver or draughtsman.

The younger Pearce's virtuosity and the range of his talents make it difficult to summarise his career. Architectural stone carving, wood-carving and design came early and continued until the end of his life, as did the design, and probably carving, of church monuments. Early in his career, in 1660, when perhaps no more than twenty-five years old, he was involved in the design of the triumphal arches erected for the coronation of Charles II (see p. 38). In 1665 (which is also the date of completion of Pembroke chapel) he is recorded as having carried out stone carving under Sir Roger Pratt for Lord Alington's house at Horseheath Hall, Cambridgeshire.[51] By this time he

---

50 Ibid., 46.
51 R T Gunther, *The architecture of Sir Roger Pratt* (Oxford, 1928), 130.

must have had a certain reputation. His sculptures range from about 1671 to almost the end of his life.[52]

Pearce was to be closely associated with Wren for much of his career. From 1671, following the Great Fire, they worked together on seven of the City churches, for four of which Pearce was the master mason, as well as doing much carving in wood and stone. In 1676 he was paid for his designs for Wren's Emmanuel College chapel, where he returned to do carving in 1687. In September 1678 he became one of the four master masons initially appointed for the building of St Paul's Cathedral and worked there until 1691 as mason and stone carver, concentrating mainly on the south transept and portico.[53] In 1686–87, towards the end of his life, he designed and built the Bishop's Palace at Lichfield, for which he also did stone carving. This was his only known completed architectural commission. He made many designs for funeral monuments that he or his workshop executed. Ultimately he had a large and thriving business, based in London where most of his work was done, but with commissions coming from (among numerous other places) Cambridge, Cassiobury Park (Hertfordshire), Chester, Arkesden (Essex), Oxford, Whitkirk (Yorkshire), Sudbury Hall (Derbyshire), Wolseley Hall (Staffordshire) and Winchester College.

The esteem in which Pearce was held after his death is shown in a letter of John Talman, writing from Rome in the summer of 1711 to his father, William Talman, who worked with Pearce at Chatsworth and acquired many of his drawings after his death:

> Last Monday I had an entertainment which is the talk of the town. . . . I had the best musick in Rome composed on purpose, and a poem of above four hundred verses composed for this occasion in praise of arts and commending sevral persons there present, who were all the top virtuosi in Rome both for learning and arts. There was the chief painter, architect, sculptor, medalist, &c. in Rome, with some of the most eminent persons for learning. Round [one of the rooms] were twelve heads painted representing Vitruvius, Fabius the painter, Glycon the sculptor; opposite were Palladio, Rafael and Bonarota; on another side Inigo Jones, Fuller and Pierce; at the upper part were Horace the poet, Rossius the comedian and Ismenia a singer, with abundance of mottos in Latin and Italian &c.[54]

---

52 A terracotta bust of Milton at Christ's College, Cambridge, for which Gunnis gives a date of *c.*1656, appears to be his earliest known work. The fact that he was 'made free by patrimony' of the Painter-Stainers' Company in that year does not necessarily imply artistic achievement by that date.

53 Eventually there were to be thirteen master masons working there. See James Campbell, *Building St Paul's* (London, 2007) and Gordon Higgott, 'The revised design for St Paul's Cathedral, 1685–90: Wren, Hawksmoor and Les Invalides', *Burlington magazine*, 146 (2004) 534–47, in which Pearce is discussed on pp. 537–8.

54 Quoted from *Wren Society*, 17, 4–5. (Original letter, MSS Marquis of Bath at Longleat, Royal Commission on Historical Manuscripts, vol. 2, 179–80).

CONTEXT

The original buildings of Pembroke College, completed by about 1385, consisted of a single small court (Old Court) situated at what is now the corner of Pembroke Street and Trumpington Street, with the original chapel in the north-west corner (Fig. 2). This is the College that Matthew Wren would have known as an undergraduate. It survived largely unaltered until 1875, when, by the demolition of its south range, Old Court became half of the present First Court.

The new chapel can be seen as part of a second building campaign of the seventeenth century. This began with the building, to the east of Old Court, of the north and south sides of what is now called Ivy Court, also shown in Loggan's engraving. Work started here on the north side with a range of rooms along Pembroke Street, the western two-thirds of which were probably built in 1614–16 and the remainder completed only in 1670, when the land became available. For this last part of the range the mason was Robert Grumbold.[55] Before that, in 1659, work began on the south range, parallel to the first and largely completed by 1661. The design of this second range (Hitcham Building) is attributed to Peter Mills.[56] It appears to be of one build but consists of two stylistically distinct sections. The eastern end, the first to be built, closely follows the modest Jacobean pattern of the other side of the court, but the north front of the western part forms a distinctive and more complex architectural composition. This represents the first appearance in Pembroke of Classical architectural features, employed in the artisan mannerist style that Mills used elsewhere. In this part of the building, a large room on the first floor (now called the Thomas Gray Room) was apparently roughly plastered but not yet panelled at the time when the chapel was being built. As will appear, this room is of particular significance in the building history of the chapel.

The new chapel, consecrated in 1665, came next in these seventeenth-century developments. Twenty-five years later, in 1690, conversion of the old chapel into a library was completed. The splendid room thus created, now called the Old Library, is discussed in Appendix 2.

---

55 RCHM, *Cambridge,* part 2, 154; PCA, Treasury Accounts, vol. 2, 157.
56 Howard Colvin, 'Thorpe Hall and its architect', in *Essays in English architectural history* (New Haven and London, 1999), 158–78. See also RCHM, *Cambridge,* part 2, 148 and pl. 212.

Ivy Court gives the impression of having been devised piecemeal, without the intention of creating a new formal court. Its two modest ranges would have made a difficult and unsatisfactory context for the interpolation of a new, wholly Classical chapel, for which east–west orientation was mandatory according to Laudian precepts.[57] A chapel here would also not have been visible from the street, important if its supposed symbolic purpose was to be achieved. Fortunately, the College owned land to the south of Old Court, fronting onto Trumpington Street. This site had disadvantages, in that it was not immediately accessible from Old Court and was largely hidden to view from the rest of the College (Fig. 2). Notwithstanding these drawbacks, this became the site of the new chapel. At some time in 1662 the College redeemed a recently granted lease of St Thomas' Hostel, which occupied part of the site, and demolished it.[58] By this date, then, the location of the new chapel must have been decided. The decision to build the new chapel was therefore presumably taken between March 1660, when Matthew Wren was released from captivity, and an unknown date in 1662.

[57] At Emmanuel College, Cambridge, the new chapel, also designed by Wren, was built to replace the existing chapel, which was in the unacceptable north–south orientation. See Stubbings, *Emmanuel College chapel*, 4.

[58] Willis and Clark, vol. 1, 44.

DESIGN: STAGES AND SOURCES

The College's records reveal nothing about how the Master and Fellows dealt with Matthew Wren when he offered to fund the building of a new chapel. Would they have taken the initiative in suggesting an architect, or was Matthew Wren in control? Knowing what we do of him, it seems unlikely that the bishop would have left the matter wholly in the College's hands – indeed, it seems highly probable that at some point he may have taken the lead, for the College itself would hardly have hit upon Christopher Wren, unknown at the time as an architect. But if Wren was ultimately to be chosen, he was almost certainly not first in the field. This much can be deduced from the one major surviving piece of documentary evidence about the history of the chapel's design.

The preliminary drawing

In the College's archives there is an undated, unsigned drawing showing a preliminary design for a side elevation of a chapel-like building (Fig. 7). This was among Matthew Wren's papers brought to Pembroke after his death, an important reason for associating it with the chapel. Minns and Webb, who first published it, wrote that this 'is almost certainly a tentative design [for the chapel] by Wren'.[59] They are correct as to the first suggestion but not in attributing it to Wren: who made the drawing will become apparent.

The drawing shows a façade of five bays, divided by stone pilaster strips,[60] with a round-headed window in each bay. There is no indication of the adoption of any Classical order. The pilaster strips, lacking capitals, break into a heavy modillion cornice (that is, a cornice in which the bottom band is formed of a row of separate blocks of stone or wood) and are continued above this into what appears to be a continuous blank parapet, where each is topped by a pineapple- or cone-shaped finial. The roof (not drawn) would have sloped down to end behind the parapet. The bases of the pilaster strips are integrated into a continuous plinth. The windows have stone framing, without keystones; the sills are supported by brackets, as are the straight cornices above. Panels below the windows, a prominent feature of the chapel as built (Fig. 5), are not present.

---

59   E H Minns and M E Webb, 'Pembroke College Chapel, Cambridge: Sir Christopher Wren's first building', in Rudolf Dircks (ed.), *Sir Christopher Wren, A.D. 1632–1723: bicentenary memorial volume* (London, 1923), 229–32.

60   'Pilaster strip' is the technical term for a pilaster without base or capital.

THE SEVENTEENTH-CENTURY CHAPEL

7. Preliminary study for the north elevation of the chapel, now attributed to Edward Pearce. Compare with Figure **5.** There are five bays instead of four and the pilaster strips between them were not built. The idea of a balustrade above the cornice also did not survive. The windows are essentially as built (*cf.* Fig. 24). The row of pineapples (or pine cones) became the flaming urns on the corners of the chapel. The doorway is shown with a lugged architrave and a cornice above it cutting into the window, features that did not survive. (Pembroke College Architectural Archive.)

8. Old St Paul's cathedral, detail of transept as remodelled by Inigo Jones; compare with Figure 7. From a drawing by Christopher Wren for an unexecuted scheme for remodelling the pre-fire cathedral. The drawing dates from 1666, i.e. after Pembroke chapel was built. (All Souls College, Oxford; Geraghty, *Architectural drawings*, no. 46.)

In the right-hand bay there is a stone-framed doorway, where the chapel door would eventually be. However, the cornice above the doorway cuts awkwardly through the sill of the window above and at first sight this doorway looks like an afterthought, the draughtsman perhaps belatedly realising that the chapel would need an entrance, that this could not be on the west front (since this would have necessitated leaving the College and walking along the street to get in), and that, given the position of the chapel in the College, the door would have to be on the north side. However, apart from this doorway, there is nothing in the drawing to indicate whether this is a north or south elevation: at this early stage, the draughtsman may have been economising in effort and using it to show both the south side, with five windows, and, by addition of the doorway, the appearance of the north side. Whether there could be any sort of window above the doorway would at this stage have been problematic, since the question of how the chapel might be brought into relationship with adjacent buildings had not been addressed: as we shall see, until quite late in the design process the chapel was thought of as free-standing.

A significant feature of the drawing, helping to confirm that it is indeed related to Pembroke chapel, is that from the scale on the drawing the building would have been approximately 78 feet long, corresponding closely to that of the built chapel, which can be ascertained from Scott's survey drawing (Fig. 4). This length was almost certainly determined by an external factor that had already been taken into account by those thinking about the new chapel. Loggan's engraving (Fig. 2) shows a channel conveying water into the College running along the south side of the chapel. This was a tributary of Hobson's Conduit (or the 'Cambridge New River'), which brought water to the town from springs to the south. The branch entering Pembroke almost certainly pre-dated the chapel. Initially an open channel, it ran first eastwards along what is now the south side of the chapel and then (now enclosed) veered north.[61] The point at which it turned north is revealed in a letter of 1879 from the College to G G Scott, who was then planning the extension to the chapel, in which the Bursar tells him that 'Hobson's Conduit runs beneath the ground immediately to the east of the present Chapel'.[62] This seems likely to have determined where the east end of the new chapel could lie. The draughtsman must therefore have known both where the chapel was to be built and also this important constraint about the site. Given that building began in May 1663, the drawing must obviously have been made prior to that, but it is not possible to date it with any certainty for, although the site was procured some time in 1662, it could have been decided on prior to that date.

While the drawing indicates the eventual length of the chapel, the height – 25 feet 4 inches to the bottom of the cornice – is considerably less than that

---

61 It went on to pass under Ivy Court and into Pembroke Street; see W D Bushell, *Hobson's Conduit* (Cambridge, 1938), 37–9.
62 Letter of C H Prior to G G Scott, 24 October 1879 (RIBA Collection, SC/CA/PC/202).

of the chapel as built (32 feet). The height shown in the drawing would have been close to that of the old chapel. It will be shown later (pp. 52–4) that such a height would have been incompatible with the eventual treatment of the west front.

Although the drawing does not show the chapel as it was built, it does contain some of the principal features of the eventual side elevations. There are the same round-headed windows with straight cornices above; like the sills, these are supported on brackets. The row of finials can be seen as precursors of the four flaming urns now on the corners of the building. The pilaster strips shown in the drawing became Corinthian pilasters, though placed only at the corners of the building, rather than between every bay. Additionally, the length of the chapel appears to have been decided. The drawing is evidently a key document, and its place in the design history of the chapel – the sources it draws on and the identity of the draughtsman – must now be discussed.

The source of the design, although on a quite different scale, can be found in the elevation of the nave aisles and transepts of old St Paul's cathedral (Fig. 8).[63] This was the work of Inigo Jones, who between 1631 and 1642 remodelled the Gothic cathedral in Classical style. Here again, there are round-headed windows with straight cornices above. Between them (concealing Romanesque buttresses) are ashlared pilaster strips which, as in the chapel drawing, break into a modillion cornice and continue through a plain parapet to be capped by pineapple finials. The similarities here are very close. Jones may have adopted pilaster strips, without capitals or bases, to harmonise with the Gothic of the underlying cathedral, a subtlety of which the draughtsman of the preliminary Pembroke elevation may have been unaware when he repeated the pilaster strips for what was to be a Classical building.[64] To establish this source for the preliminary drawing is not altogether surprising, for Jones's work would inescapably have been the major English influence on any architect of the time designing a Classical chapel. In the Queen's Chapel at St James's Palace (1623–5) and in St Paul's church, Covent Garden (1631–3) Jones had already provided the models for the deployment of the Classical style in English protestant church architecture.

The identification of this probable source of the design shown in the drawing prompted a search for further indications of a Jonesian influence, particularly in the light of Wittkower's view that 'Inigo Jones, a true descendant of the humanist tradition, founded his theoretical deliberations on the metaphysical belief in the universal efficacy and beauty of numbers'.[65] Toplis

---

63 This was pointed out to me by Gordon Higgott. For Jones's work at old St Paul's see John Summerson, *Inigo Jones* (Harmondsworth, 1964) and John Summerson, 'Inigo Jones', in *The unromantic castle*, 41–62.
64 I owe this suggestion to Geoffrey Fisher.
65 Rudolf Wittkower, *Architectural principles in the age of humanism*, 5th edn (London, 1998), 143; see also Wittkower, 'Inigo Jones, architect and man of letters', in *Palladio and English Palladianism* (London, 1974).

DESIGN: STAGES AND SOURCES

Ratios in the preliminary drawing

Fig. 9 shows one bay of the preliminary drawing of the north elevation, on which twelve dimensions (labelled *a* to *l*) have been measured in mm. There are slight differences in these dimensions in the five bays, possibly resulting from uneven shrinkage of the paper during conservation: the dimensions given in the table are averages over the whole drawing. The corresponding length of each dimension in feet (derived by using the scale bar on the drawing) is given in the table in brackets.

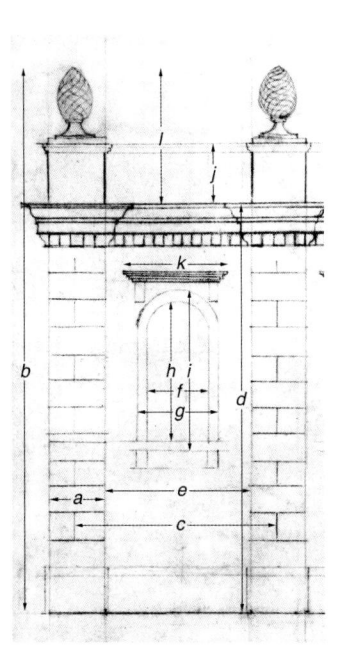

9. One bay of the preliminary drawing (Fig. 7), to show the dimensions used in calculating the ratios in the table.

Dimension	mm. (feet)	exact ratio	ratio rounded off
Overall length of elevation Overall height, to top of finials* (*b*)	348 (78) 175 (39)	1.99:1	**2:1**
Overall height, to top of finials* (*b*) Width of pilaster strip (*a*)	175 (40) 17.5 (4)	10:1	**10:1**
Height of bay, to top of cornice (*d*) Width of bay, including 1 pilaster strip (*c*)	130 (29) 66 (15)	1.97:1	**2:1**
Width of bay, including 1 pilaster strip (*c*) Height of window, without framing (*f*)	66 (15) 44 (10)	3:2	**3:2**
Height of window, including framing (*i*) Width of window, including framing (*g*)	52 (12) 27 (6)	1.93:1	**2:1**
Height of window, including framing (*i*) Width of pilaster strip (*a*)	52 (12) 17.5 (4)	2.97:1	**3:1**
Width of window, including framing (*g*) Width of pilaster strip (*a*)	27 (6) 17.5 (4)	3:1.94	**3:2**
Height of parapet (*j*) Width of pilaster strip (*a*)	19 (4) 17.5 (4)	1.09:1	**1:1**
Width of window cornice (*k*) Width of pilaster strip (*a*)	35.5 (8) 17.5 (4)	2.03:1	**2:1**
Top of cornice to top of finial (*l*) Height of window, without framing (*h*)	44 (10) 44 (10)	1:1	**1:1**
Internal width of bay (*e*) Height of window, without framing (*h*)	44 (10) 44 (10)	1:1	**1:1**

* This measurement is made to a faint survey line framing the elevation. The finials themselves vary slightly in height.

33

had reported that 'analysis of the designs of [Jones's] major works demonstrates conclusively the immanence of the harmonic proportions', and in support listed a series of ratios of increasing complexity, beginning with 1:1, 2:1 and 3:2.[66] The belief referred to by Wittkower goes back to the Renaissance architectural theorists, whom Jones had attentively studied. Measurements were therefore made on the drawing (Fig. 9) and revealed that many of the dimensions are related to each other in simple ratio – 1:1, 2:1, 3:1, 3:2 and 10:1. Eleven instances are listed in the accompanying table.

These ratios apply both to individual architectural elements – the bays, for example, are twice as high as wide, the pilaster strips ten times – and to the spacings between these elements. The drawing appears in some respects to be largely an exercise in achieving simple mathematical relationships between all parts of an elevation and the extent to which this aim is achieved is no mean accomplishment. Many of the dimensions used in the drawing translate, to a close approximation, into whole, mostly even, numbers of feet: 2, 4, 6, 8, 10, 12 and 15. The choice of these (which have no particular architectural rationale) would have simplified the draughtsman's task and would appear to be part of his strategy for achieving the resultant mathematical harmony. The draughtsman must surely have been acquainted either with Inigo Jones's work or that of his followers, and we will return to this point.

A curious feature of the drawing, unexpected in an architectural design and not readily explicable, is a slanting line running down at a shallow angle from left to right (east to west, if this is viewed as a north elevation). The line is clearly defined only where it traverses the pilaster strips and its careful restriction to these places suggests that it is not a result of careless draughtsmanship. At its left-hand end it begins at the level of the tops of the window sills; at the mid-point of the elevation – the centre of the third bay – it intersects the centre of the bottom of the window sill. It ends fairly exactly on top of the fourth course of stone of the right-hand pilaster strip, passing en route closely over the architrave of the adjacent door, the height of which it might conceivably be taken to determine. Otherwise no convincing explanation for this line has so far suggested itself. It is tempting to suppose that, in some as yet unexplained way, it formed part of the draughtsman's attempt to bring all parts of the design into simple mathematical relationship.

We have so far spoken of 'the draughtsman' who was responsible for this drawing and the reader may by this time be wondering why, if Wren was the architect of the chapel, it should not be he who drew the elevation. He was, after all, thoroughly familiar by this time with Inigo Jones's work at old St Paul's. The drawing used here to illustrate Jones's work there (Fig. 8) is by

---

66 G Toplis, 'The sources of Jones's mind and imagination', in J Harris, S Orgel and R Strong., *The King's Arcadia: Inigo Jones and the Stuart court* (London, 1973) 61–3. For a more recent discussion see Gordon Higgott, 'Varying with reason: Inigo Jones's theory of design', *Architectural History*, 35 (1992), 51–77.

DESIGN: STAGES AND SOURCES

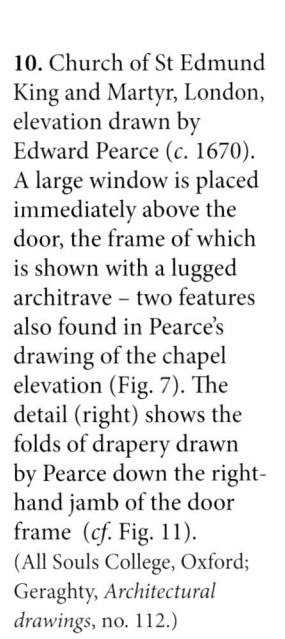

10. Church of St Edmund King and Martyr, London, elevation drawn by Edward Pearce (*c.* 1670). A large window is placed immediately above the door, the frame of which is shown with a lugged architrave – two features also found in Pearce's drawing of the chapel elevation (Fig. 7). The detail (right) shows the folds of drapery drawn by Pearce down the right-hand jamb of the door frame (*cf*. Fig. 11).
(All Souls College, Oxford; Geraghty, *Architectural drawings*, no. 112.)

Wren and, although it was not made until 1666 (as part of his scheme for a dome over the crossing of the old cathedral), he had been asked to advise the king on possible repairs to the cathedral as early as the autumn of 1661.[67] However, quite apart from the quality of the draughtsmanship, which is inferior to what might be expected from Wren even at this stage of his career, there is now positive evidence that he did not make the Pembroke drawing.

Study by Anthony Geraghty and Gordon Higgott of drawings in the All Souls, Oxford collection of Wren-associated material has revealed two, relating to London City churches, which contain significant details resembling those of the preliminary drawing. Both of these drawings have been previously published: one is an elevation of St Edmund King and Martyr (Fig. 10);[68] the other is a design now probably to be associated with St Lawrence Jewry.[69] In all three drawings, immediately below a round-headed window

67 Kerry Downes, *Sir Christopher Wren: the design of St. Paul's cathedral* (London, 1988), 9. See also Gordon Higgott 'The fabric to 1670' in D Keene *et al.* (eds), *St Paul's: the cathedral church of London, 604–2004* (New York and London, 2004), 171–90.
68 Anthony Geraghty, *The architectural drawings of Sir Christopher Wren at All Souls College, Oxford* (Aldershot, 2007), 86, no. 112; AS II, 44. (Also in *Wren Society*, 9, pl. 15.)
69 Geraghty, *Architectural drawings*, 87, no. 113; AS I, 60. (Also *Wren Society*, 9, pl. 33, bottom left.)

11. Door-case from Dunster Castle, probably by Edward Pearce. Compare the descending folds of drapery down the left side with those in Figure 10. (National Trust.)

there is a square-headed doorway with a wide straight cornice: in both design and draughtsmanship the three drawings are here closely linked. There are also resemblances in points of detail between the preliminary drawing and the St Edmund King and Martyr elevation: in both the architrave of the doorway extends laterally beyond the jambs; the tops of the pilaster strips break awkwardly into the cornices, with the dentils of the cornice running across them. Flaming urns and/or pineapple finials occur in all three drawings.

The two All Souls drawings have recently been identified as the work of Edward Pearce. These attributions are based on the typical, somewhat free draughtsmanship, comparable to that in, for example, Pearce's designs for church monuments and architectural details[70] and also (more objectively) on the characteristic writing of the numbers on the scale bars, which Higgott has shown can be reliably used to identify particular draughtsmen.[71] Pearce is also linked to the St Lawrence Jewry drawing by the fact that he worked there as mason.[72] Both churches come at the beginning of the campaign to re-build the City churches, which must date the drawings to the early 1670s. A perhaps telling connection is that close inspection of the elevation for St Edmund King and Martyr reveals descending folds of drapery drawn down the right-hand side of the door frame, a detail repeated on some interior

---

70 For example, those in the Soane Museum collection (*Soane*, vol. 3, nos 60, 61, 62, 64 and 68).

71 Higgott, 'The revised design'. This paper makes extensive use of the writing of numerals in the identification of draughtsmen, including Pearce and Wren.

72 Paul Jeffery, *The City churches of Sir Christopher Wren* (London, 1996), 253–5.

door-cases at Dunster Castle (Fig. 11), almost certainly Pearce's work and dating from alterations made there in 1680.

If it is accepted that these All Souls drawings were made by Pearce it is difficult to avoid the conclusion that he also made the Pembroke drawing. Apart from the similarities in design, the numbers on the scale on the Pembroke drawing closely resemble those on the All Souls drawings and other known Pearce drawings.[73] Another similarity is that in the preliminary drawing, as is frequently the case in Pearce's drawings (for example, the design for a Corinthian capital for St Paul's (Fig. 60), discussed later), the scale bar itself is drawn as a double line. If the draughtsmanship in other Pearce drawings is freer than that in the Pembroke drawing, this may well result from the fact that, in the latter, Pearce (assuming now his authorship) was working through a mathematical exercise rather than designing freely.

This is the first piece of evidence to be presented here (or, indeed, anywhere) that Edward Pearce worked on Pembroke chapel. As already noted, there is no documentary evidence to show how he might first have become involved with this project or how an architect was eventually appointed. Some speculations are, however, in order.

The possibility that Pearce was simply acting as a draughtsman for Christopher Wren is unlikely. The characteristic features of the drawing that allow it to be attributed to Pearce and which would reappear in his later designs, do not seem to find any place in Wren's subsequent work and would therefore not have originated with him. On balance, it seems probable that Pearce made the chapel drawing before Wren was involved. At this early stage, Pearce might have been working, if not with Wren, then for or with another architect, or he could have been acting independently. This last possibility is worth considering, for Pearce certainly had architectural ambitions. His only known completed building, the Bishop's Palace at Lichfield, dating from 1686–87, came late in his life, but he made designs for other buildings: a drawing in his hand survives for an elevation of a house that was to have been built in about 1676 on the site of Norfolk House, in the Strand, London.[74] Throughout his career, he provided designs for parts of buildings: cornices, door-cases, chapel stalls, gate piers and much else. These architectural interests probably came about from his father's association with Inigo Jones. Even if the younger Pearce did not actually come into contact with Jones (or with his nephew and pupil, John Webb), his ideas would have filtered down to him. A Jonesian influence on the Pembroke drawing is therefore understandable. As already noted, Matthew Wren would very probably also have known

---

73　An anomaly must be noted here: in the Pembroke drawing the '8' is drawn most unusually, with a straight, horizontal top. It seems likely that the draughtsman, having written the preceding '7', began to write another, realised his mistake and converted it into an '8'. I am grateful to Michael Reeve for suggesting this explanation.

74　Colvin, *Biographical dictionary*, 792.

Jones through his connection with the Stuart court, and might well have been acquainted with one or both of the Pearces. Jones died in 1652 and the elder Pearce in 1658 – both, that is, while Matthew Wren was still in the Tower and presumably before the new Pembroke chapel was in prospect. Because of his acquaintance with them, however, Matthew Wren, after his release, might well have turned first to the younger Pearce for ideas about the design of his new chapel.

An alternative scenario, suggested by Geoffrey Fisher, can also be proposed.[75] Hitcham Building, the south range of Ivy Court at Pembroke, built between 1659 and 1661, is attributed to Peter Mills, who at that time could well have been regarded as the College's architect. When the possibility of the new chapel arose, the fellows might first have been minded to turn to him. There are indications that Mills was on good terms with Pembroke. He held three London tenements under a lease from the College granted in April 1662 and due to expire in 1702; when these were destroyed in the Great Fire, the College, in consideration of his great loss, agreed in 1668 to extend the lease for a further thirty-four years, on condition that he rebuilt the houses 'with all convenient speed'.[76] Mills had a substantial reputation as surveyor, as well as architect. Along with Wren, Hugh May and Sir Roger Pratt, he was one of those appointed after the Fire to supervise the rebuilding of the City. Before working for Pembroke, he was responsible for Thorpe Hall, near Peterborough, his most important building, which he designed in 1653–54 for Oliver St John, Chief Justice during the Commonwealth.[77] He probably also designed the very similar Wisbech Castle for John Thurloe, Cromwell's Secretary of State. There is stylistic evidence that the younger Pearce played a significant part in the interior decoration of Thorpe Hall, the carving of the balustrade of the main staircase, in particular, closely resembling that of Sudbury Hall, Derbyshire (known to be by Pearce). The date of Pearce's work at Thorpe Hall is not certainly known but is likely to have been before the Restoration in 1660. A further connection between Mills and Pearce has recently been established. For the coronation of Charles II on 22 April 1661 four large temporary arches were built for the king's entry into the City and Mills was one of the designers of these. In his contemporary description of the arches, John Ogilby tells us that Mills worked 'with another Person, who desires to have his Name conceal'd'.[78] Drawings for the arches survive and have recently been identified by Geoffrey Fisher as being in Pearce's hand, who was, therefore, in all probability (rather than Sir Balthazar Gerbier, as formerly

---

75 Personal communication, September 2008.
76 Colvin, *Biographical dictionary*, 3rd edn, 656. The latter part of this sentence is omitted from the 4th edn.
77 Colvin, 'Thorpe Hall'.
78 John Ogilby, *The relation of His Majestie's entertainment passing through the City of London to his coronation: with a description of the triumphal arches, and solemnity* (London, 1661), 39.

surmised), the person desirous of anonymity.[79] Why should Pearce have wished to conceal his role in this work? Fisher makes the plausible suggestion that Mills's Cromwellian associations would have made him unacceptable to Matthew Wren as architect for his new chapel. The College might nevertheless have consulted Mills, who could have recommended his multi-talented young associate, Pearce, whom the College in turn proposed to the bishop. In this case, Pearce would understandably have wanted his association with Mills to be kept secret in Ogilby's book, the two editions of which in 1661 and 1662 appeared just when the bishop's thoughts would have turned to the new chapel.

There is no way of knowing how far Pearce progressed with his design. The likely reason for his displacement as the chapel's architect is simply that Christopher Wren found himself increasingly drawn to architecture and made his interest known to his uncle. Pearce stayed on, it will be argued, in a subsidiary role as an assisting designer and carver. To link himself in this way to an architect was eventually to be the strategy of Pearce's career: apart from Mills and Wren, he worked with Sir Roger Pratt at Horseheath, with William Winde at Combe Abbey and Hampstead Marshall and with William Talman at Chatsworth.[80]

*

After the preliminary drawing, the next piece of evidence we have about the design process of the chapel is in the form of a wooden model that represents a very late stage in the design. The gap between it and the drawing is large and there is no clue as to how this was bridged. As will be shown, there is one definite indication, in a point of detail, that Wren was responsible for the model.

The model

Like the preliminary drawing, the model (Figs 12, 13, 14) was first described by Minns and Webb.[81] Wren seems to have made use of Pearce's drawing for ideas about the side elevations but (unless Pearce made studies, now lost, for the other façades) drew on other sources for the rest of the design. What these were will be discussed shortly.

The strongly visual component in Wren's thinking has already been noted. He had made use of models in his scientific studies from an early age and it would probably have seemed natural for him to do so when he came to architecture. Models were made for the Sheldonian Theatre and for Emmanuel College chapel.[82] The Pembroke chapel model almost certainly came

79 For discussion of the arches see Christine Stevenson, 'Occasional architecture in seventeenth-century London', *Architectural History*, 49 (2006), 35–74.
80 See Colvin, *Biographical dictionary*, 791–3; Eustace, 'Pearce, Edward'.
81 Minns and Webb, 'Pembroke chapel'. See also Kerry Downes, *Sir Christopher Wren: an exhibition selected by Kerry Downes at the Whitechapel Art Gallery* (London, 1982), 52.
82 Neither of these models survives. The Emmanuel College chapel model cost over £13 (Stubbings, *Emmanuel College chapel*, 9).

12. Wooden model of the chapel, from the north west, with a round window (not built) above the door; height 37 cm, length 68 cm, width 30 cm. (Paul Whitehead, 2009)

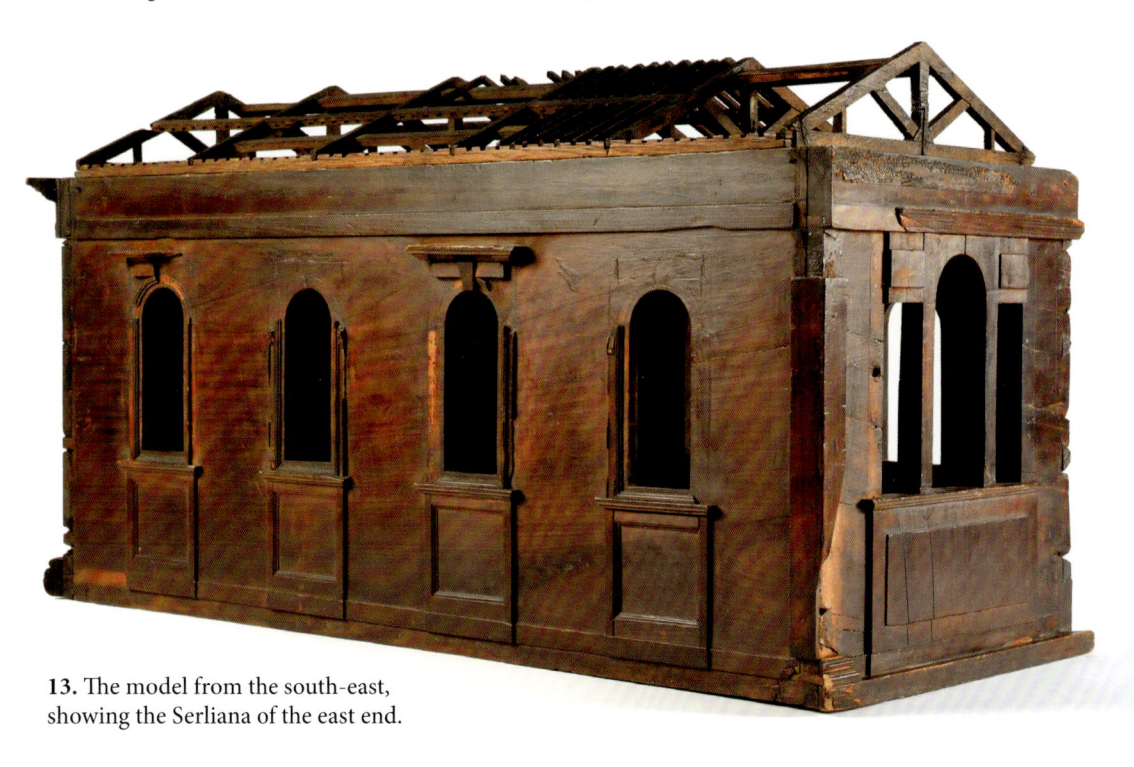

13. The model from the south-east, showing the Serliana of the east end.

DESIGN: STAGES AND SOURCES

14. Roof trusses in the model. The arrow indicates a metal strap. (James Austin, c.1993)

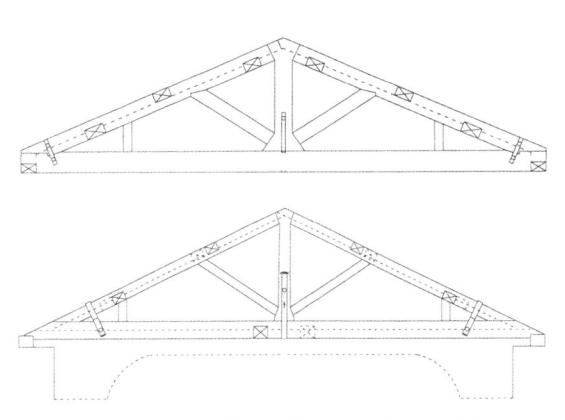

15. Comparison of a roof truss in the model (above) with that in the chapel as built. (Drawings by James Campbell.)

before both of these and is the humble first antecedent, therefore, of Wren's Great Model for St Paul's cathedral, large enough to be walked about in.

The model is mostly of cedar, with roof timbers of oak. Neatly made dovetail joints at the corners suggest that it was the work of a cabinet-maker. It has suffered a good deal of loss and damage, particularly of decorative features. However, the position of missing elements, such as some of the pilasters on the west front, is clear from differences in the colour of the wood. Parts of some of the pilaster capitals are present and show that a Corinthian order was to be used: the building has become overtly Classical. Wren's use of the Corinthian order was innovatory, the only previous example of its use in English church architecture being the church of St Katherine Cree (1628–31) in the City of London.[83] Three pilaster bases, or parts of them, also survive and are of particular consequence for this study, as will be seen. The entablature and pediment of the west front are almost all missing. The roof covering (probably originally removable) is also lacking, but enough of the roof timbers remain to show how they were to be constructed. The overall proportions of the model are precisely those of the chapel as built.[84]

The model would have served several purposes. One was presumably to allow Wren to study in three dimensions what he was proposing to build. Another would have been to show Bishop Wren and the Master and Fellows of Pembroke what the new chapel would look like. A third – and this was seemingly of particular importance – was to guide the builders, for the model was made with an attention to detail that went beyond anything needed for the other purposes. James Campbell's comparison of the roof structure of the chapel with that of the model shows exact correspondence between the two

83 John Newman, 'Laudian literature and the interpretation of Caroline churches in London', in David Howarth (ed.), *Art and patronage in the Caroline courts* (Cambridge, 1993), 179.
84 The dimensions of Wren's chapel can be obtained from Scott's surveys.

in design and dimensions (Fig. 15).[85] The roof trusses of the model, every one of which was apparently originally present, are made precisely to scale, the ironwork being represented by tiny strips of metal with dots of solder to indicate bolts: the model would have enabled the carpenters to construct the roof without further information. (The type of braced king-post truss shown in the model would be used repeatedly by Wren.) The only departure from the model is that the purlins are reduced from three to two, perhaps on the advice of the carpenters. Similarly, sufficient fragments of the mouldings around the windows remain to show that the stonework was represented in the model just as it was built. To a large extent, therefore, the model could have served instead of drawings for the builders, which suggests that, although the term 'modell' might at that period refer to a drawing as well as to an actual model, it was the latter that was probably intended when it was used in the contract with the bricklayers (see p. 59).

The main difference between the preliminary drawing and the model – and the change is an extremely important one – is that the side elevations have become much higher. If the length of the model (which lacks a scale[86]) is taken to represent what was finally built, the height of the side walls (measuring to the bottom of the cornice) can be calculated as approximately 31 feet 6inches, which is close to that of the built chapel. This compares with the calculated height of 25 feet 4 inches in the preliminary drawing. The reasons for this substantial change will become apparent shortly. One consequence of the increase in height is that, if the five bays shown in the drawing had been retained, the windows would have become tall and excessively narrow; the bays are therefore reduced to four and the windows become correspondingly larger, both in height and width.

Comparison of the detailing of the windows of the side elevations in the model with those in the preliminary drawing also shows the design moving on in important ways. The increase in their size allows their framing to become wider and more complex. Keystones are now present, extending above the round heads of the windows to meet the straight cornice above (compare with Fig. 24) and the brackets supporting the cornice have become longer and more slender, all this resulting in a design intermediate between that used by Inigo Jones for old St Paul's (Fig. 8) and that shown in a drawing of his for the Queen's Chapel of Somerset House (Fig. 25). Stone-framed panels have been introduced below the windows – a feature that Wren introduced into many of his later designs and now making its first appearance.

The pilaster strips between the bays in the drawing have gone. Pilasters with Classical capitals and bases are now present, clasping the four corners of

---

85 J W P Campbell, 'Sir Christopher Wren, the Royal Society, and the development of structural carpentry 1660–1710' (unpublished PhD thesis, University of Cambridge, 2000).
86 If the length of the model (27 inches) is taken to represent the actual length of the chapel as built (78 feet, from Scott's survey drawing), the model is made at a scale of 1 inch to just under 3 feet.

the building and with two more on the west façade. The parapet shown in the drawing is no longer present and the roof timbers show that the roof was now to overhang the walls. The deep cornice of the drawing has been replaced by a lighter one. In all this and also, as we shall see, in the east and west elevations, the model shows what was built.

The pilaster bases, of which three survive, call for special attention. Gordon Higgott noticed that the mouldings on these are represented in considerable detail and merited further study. Impressions taken of them[87] show that all of the surviving pilaster bases are identical and must have been made by the same tool (Fig. 16). This could have been a miniature moulding plane or, more probably, given that cedar wood is soft and easily worked, a scraper filed to the exact profile. The detail is remarkably sharp. The prominent features of the profile – the large torus at the bottom and smaller torus at the top, with the (concave) scotia between – are standard features of the Corinthian column or pilaster base. However, the pilaster bases of the model are more complex in that there is a small convex moulding above each torus.

This more complex profile invites comparison with those on a sheet of drawings, known to be in Wren's hand, in the All Souls collection, in which he works in exploratory fashion through four versions of a pilaster base.[88] He would no doubt have taken published models as his starting point, per-

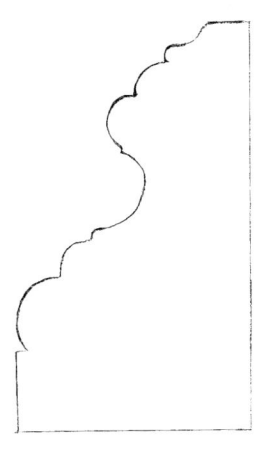

16. Profile of a pilaster base from the chapel model, drawn from a section of a mould.

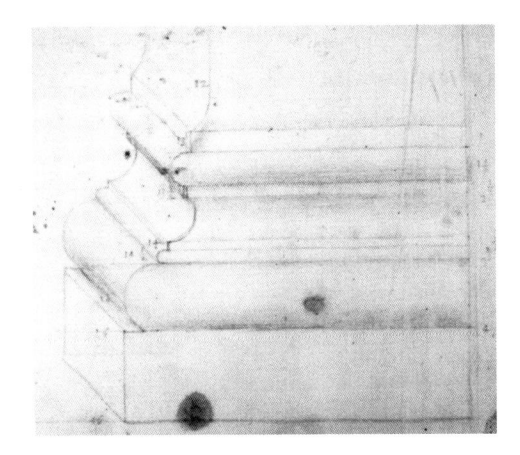

17. Pencil study by Wren for pilaster base mouldings, drawn in perspective and closely resembling the profile in Figure 16. (All Souls College, Oxford; Geraghty, *Architectural drawings*, no. 6, detail.)

87 In order to study the mouldings in detail, impressions were taken of them in dental putty, from which casts could be made. I am indebted to Lucy Skinner for her skilled assistance here. The moulds themselves could be sliced into sections, from which the profile of the mouldings could be accurately delineated.
88 Geraghty, *Architectural drawings*, 23, no. 6; AS IV, 107–8.

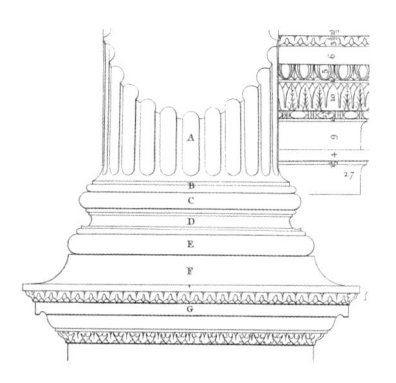

18. Corinthian pilaster base from Andrea Palladio, *Quattro libri del architettura* Book I, from Isaac Ware's English edition of 1755.

haps those in Book I of Palladio's *Quattro libri*, where he would have found a Corinthian column base such as that shown in Figure 18. He seems not to have been not entirely happy with this, perhaps finding it too complicated. Alternatives are tried, in all of which he retains from Palladio the small additional convex moulding (called a tondino), typically about one-sixth of the height of the torus, above either or both of the tori. In what was probably his final version (Fig. 17), he ended up with something rather unusual, intermediate in complexity between a typical Corinthian base and the simpler version of the Doric order. This is close to the pilaster bases of the model. Exploratory studies of this kind are exactly what one would expect of Wren at this stage of his architectural career: an experimental scientist is teaching himself the language of Classical architecture. Not all of the details in Wren's drawing could have been precisely represented in the model, for there the whole pilaster base is only 13 mm high and a tondino would have been about 0.3 mm wide and impossible to cut accurately. The small convex mouldings above the tori in the profile of the model look like an attempt on the part of the model-maker to represent them.

Since the drawings are undoubtedly Wren's, their connection with the model is evidence, hitherto lacking, for his direct and detailed involvement with the design of the chapel. Together, the drawings and the model provide a striking demonstration of his concern to achieve correct Classical detail. The pilaster drawings would appear on this evidence to be the earliest of Wren's surviving architectural designs.

The drawings had previously been tentatively connected with Pembroke College by Anthony Geraghty, but this had seemed uncertain because, in the event, the pilaster bases actually carved on the chapel are much simpler than those represented in either the model or Wren's drawings: there is no sign of the tondinos. Perhaps the masons pleaded practical constraints on what could be done.[89]

89 As will be apparent, the study of the pilaster bases owes much to Gordon Higgott and Anthony Geraghty. The present author's role has mainly been to provide accurate delineations of the mouldings on the model.

Although the model is undoubtedly a late stage of the design process, there are still some important differences between it and the chapel. In the west bay of the north side we find, instead of the large window above the doorway shown in the preliminary drawing, a smaller circular window – perhaps echoing those on Inigo Jones's side elevations of St Paul's cathedral (Fig. 8). This eliminates the clash between doorway and window but the chapel is still viewed as a free-standing building. There is also no sign of the cupola, though perhaps that was lost with the roof covering. These differences, present in a model that was to be used to specify constructional details, suggest a degree of haste, possibly improvisation, in the working out of the design. Anxiety to get ahead with building is understandable: Matthew Wren was seventy-eight years old when work began on site and the chapel was to be his burial place.

Internally, the model is neatly finished, with splayed reveals to the west and side windows.[90] The organ loft and the ante-chapel below are not represented. No details of the ceiling or other internal features are present.

Sources

By the time the model was made the essential features of the exterior of the chapel had been settled. Given the evidence of his preoccupation with the pilaster bases, the design was by this time in Wren's hands. Downes has suggested that 'There is no reason to believe that at this stage of his career Wren saw his design as a unity: rather it must have appeared to him, as it still does to us today, as an interior space with side and end walls.'[91] Indeed, Wren himself was later to write that 'In Things that are not seen at once, and have no Respect one to another, great Variety is commendable'.[92] A piecemeal approach certainly seems to have operated in the design of the exterior. The location of the chapel and its relationships to the other college buildings may have encouraged (or at least permitted) Wren to deal with the various elevations as separate entities. The west front, for example, cannot be seen from within the college, while from the street its relationship to the sides is scarcely perceptible. As Loggan's engraving shows (Fig. 2) the side elevations themselves would hardly have been visible from within the college at that time. We must now examine the sources that Wren drew on in designing the west and east façades of the chapel.

---

90 That is, the opening widens from the window to the internal face of the wall, allowing more light to enter.
91 Downes, *Architecture of Wren*, 32.
92 Wren, *Parentalia*, 352. The quotation comes from Wren's *Tract I* (see Lydia M Soo, *Wren's 'tracts' on architecture and other writings* (Cambridge, 1998), 202; Soo suggests that Wren's *Tracts* date from the mid–1670s.

The west front: Serlio. The fact that the chapel necessarily has an essentially private entrance, from within the college, means that the west front, on Trumpington Street, is purely for display. For reasons already discussed, it is by far the most elaborate part of the exterior and it is here that the Classical style is most explicit (Fig. 19). The source of the design has long been traced to an engraving in Serlio's *Architettura*. The five books of this influential work ('the principal Italian Cinquecento source book of the years before Palladio'[93]) were published separately between 1537 and 1547 and first brought together as *Tutte l'opere d'architettura et prospettiva*, published in Venice in 1584. Christopher Wren probably owned a copy of a later edition, that of 1663.[94]

The engraving on which the chapel west front is assumed to be based appears in Book III, folio 64r, with the description (in the English translation of 1611), 'The temple shown below is in Tivoli near the river and very ruined' (Fig. 20).[95] The building illustrated is the Roman Temple of the Sibyl (dating from the first to second centuries BC), located about 30 kilometres from Rome. Serlio appears to have surveyed the ruins of this temple himself and it is clear that his reconstruction is at several points conjectural. Of the front he says that there are no traces of the door or niches but he has shown it this way 'since it could certainly have been like this'. For present purposes, of course, what matters is not archaeological authenticity but what he drew. The similarities of his façade to the west front of the chapel, in both layout and proportions, are obvious: they include the triangular pediment, the Corinthian order and, in the lateral bays, the round-headed niches with recessed rectangular panels above and below. Such sunk panels would become a characteristic feature of Wren's work. Serlio drew a door with steps leading up to it, a feature that Wren could not take over since the chapel was not to be entered here. Wren inserts instead the large round-headed west window, with a recessed panel below. His plinth is lower, and the pilasters correspondingly taller.

A significant resemblance between the engraving and the chapel, perhaps pointing more decisively to the temple as the source of Wren's design than Downes allows,[96] is the similarity in the overall proportions: in both the

19. (opposite) Chapel, west front, with beginning of the cloister range to left. (From Belcher and Macartney, *Renaissance architecture*, 1901.)

---

93 Nikolaus Pevsner, *Wiltshire* (Harmondsworth, 1963), 519.
94 D J Watkin (ed.), *Sale catalogues of libraries of eminent persons*, vol. 4, Architects (London, 1972). Wren's library was inherited by his son and sold, with his son's books, in 1748. Lot 540 in the sale was a copy of Serlio's treatise of 1663, a Latin-Italian version. The catalogue does not show which books were Wren's and which his son's, but architectural books were probably Wren's. Since he was working on his first architectural commissions in 1663, one could imagine Wren hastening to acquire one of the most important of the Renaissance treatises as his new career opened. However, Serlio's book had been translated into seven languages since its first appearance, including an English version of 1611, and Wren could well have known the book before 1663.
95 See V Hart and P Hicks (eds), *Sebastiano Serlio on architecture* (New Haven and London, 1996), vol. 1, 126.
96 Downes, *Architecture of Wren*, 32 suggests that 'The pilastered single-arch triumphal structures also illustrated in Serlio are as appropriate as the Tivoli temple'.

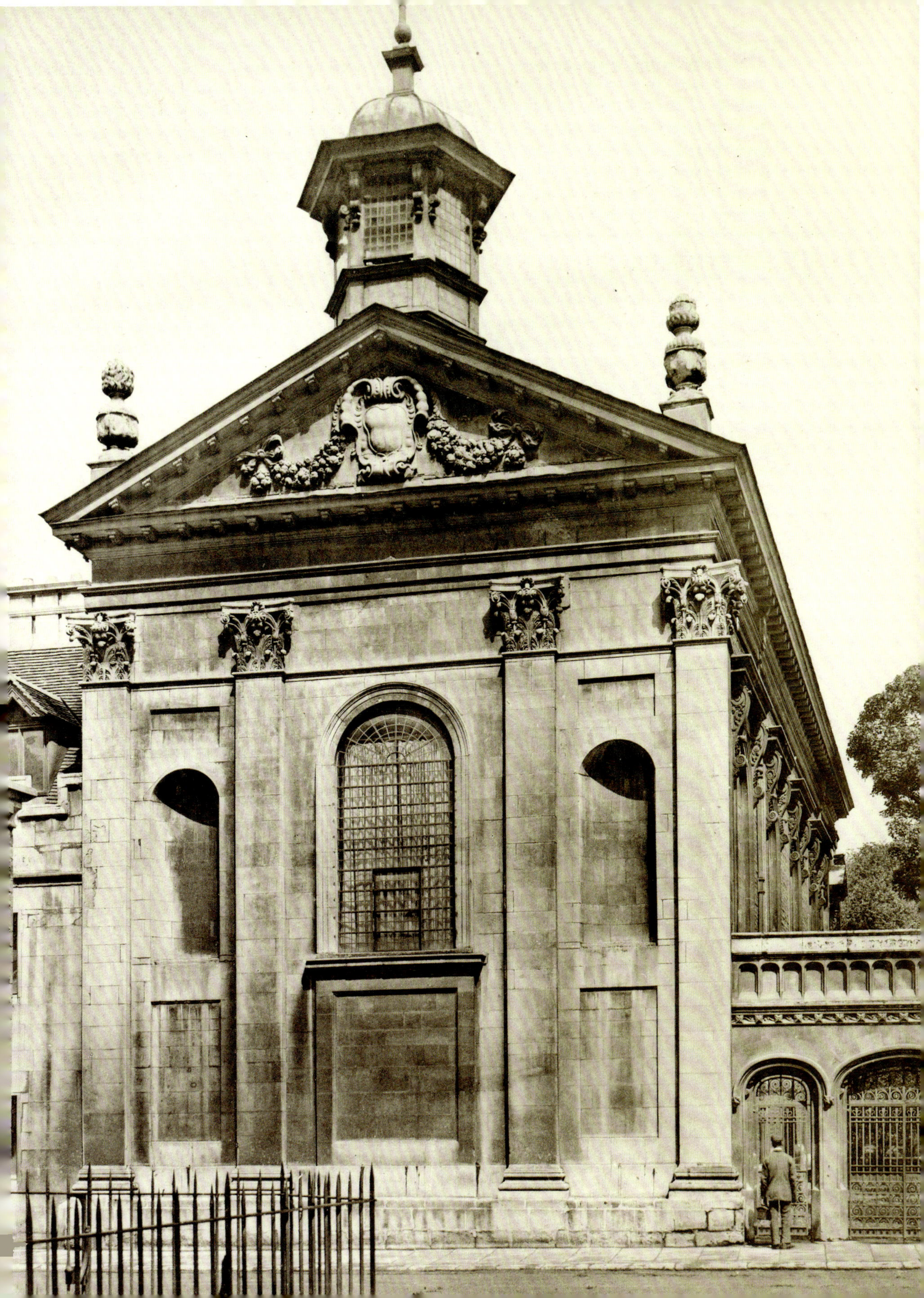

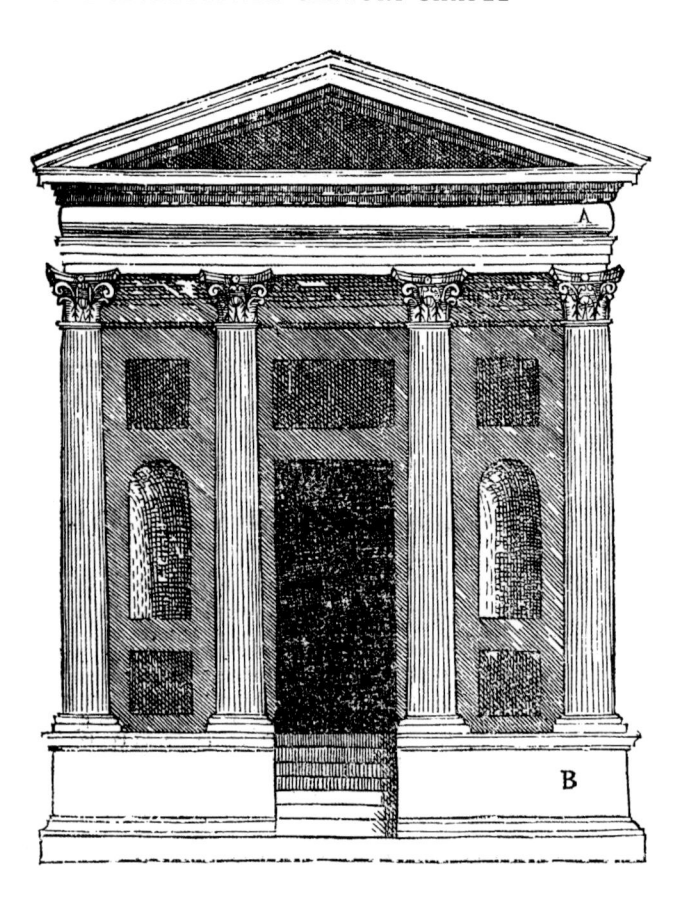

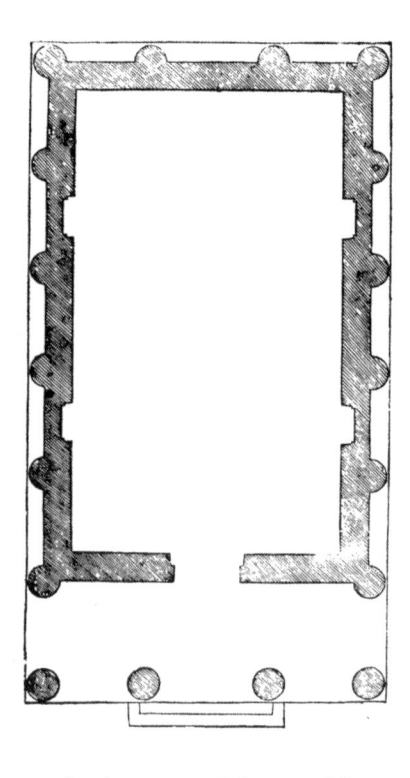

20. Serlio's reconstruction of the front elevation of the Temple of the Sibyl at Tivoli. (From Serlio, *Architettura*, Book 3, fol. 64r.)

21. Plan of the temple. The four columns supporting the portico became the pilasters of the chapel front. The temple sides are shown with five bays. (From Serlio, *Architettura*, Book 3, fol. 64v.)

engraving and the chapel, the height to the bottom of the entablature equals the width of the façade. We shall see that this particular ratio strongly influenced the overall design of the chapel.

The most important difference between the two designs is that (as others have pointed out) what might be taken for pilasters in Serlio's engraving are in fact the four columns of a portico, standing in front of the temple wall, with the pediment above them, as is made clear from his description and from the ground plan of the temple, which he gives in Book III, folio 64v (Fig. 21). As Palladio had sometimes done when incorporating a Roman temple front into the design of a villa, Wren condensed the columns into pilasters, creating what Worsley calls an implied portico.[97] Another difference is that, in Serlio's engraving, there is no carving in the pediment (cf. Fig. 19).

The plan also shows that Serlio has reconstructed the side elevations as being of five bays, separated by half-columns, the number that Pearce used in his study for the side elevation (Fig. 7). It would be interesting (but probably impossible) to know whether the resemblance is more than coincidental. The rear wall of the temple is shown without windows.

97 Giles Worsley, *Classical architecture in Britain* (New Haven and London, 1995), xii.

DESIGN: STAGES AND SOURCES

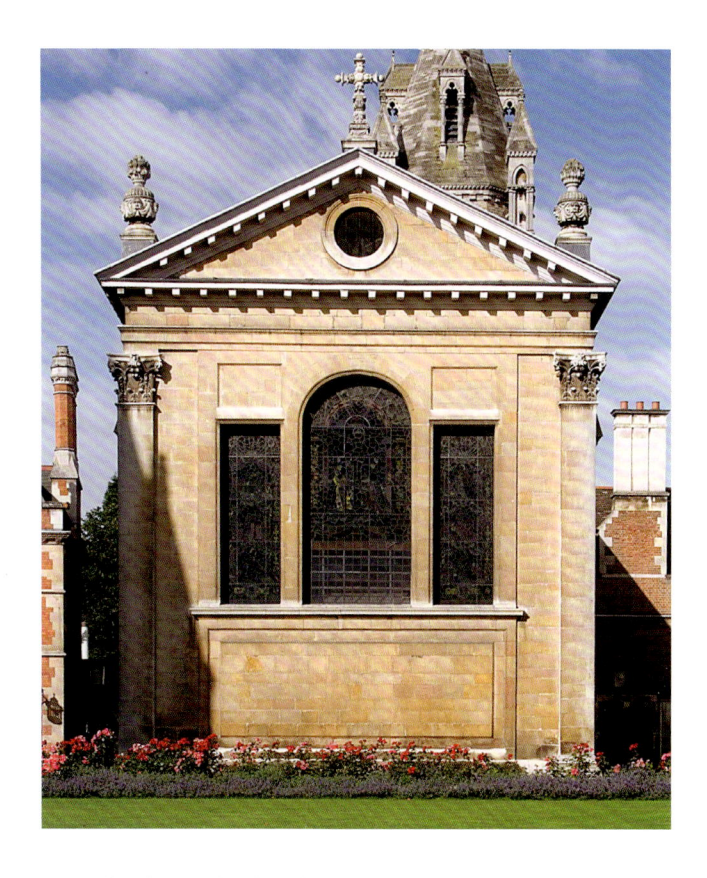

22. Chapel, east elevation. This is the original wall of the chapel, dismantled and moved eastwards by Scott. Compared with the east end of the Queen's Chapel of St James's Palace (Fig. 23), the lateral lights of the Serliana are separated from the central light by plain masonry, rather than by columns. (Ian Fleming, 2008)

In both Pembroke chapel and his almost contemporaneous Sheldonian Theatre (where his source was probably the Theatre of Marcellus), Wren drew on Roman prototypes. In this respect, as well as in seeking inspiration in Serlio, he was following Inigo Jones's example.

The east end: the Serliana. The dominant element of the east end is the three-light Serliana, a motif in which a central round-arched opening is separated (often by columns) from narrower flat-topped openings on either side. Typically, though not always, the openings are windows and it is then, in England, often called a Venetian window (Fig. 22).

In his study of Inigo Jones, Worsley argues that over a long period the Serliana was used only in important buildings, where it became symbolic of prestige and authority.[98] In Roman architecture it seems to have been used only in palaces or temples, while from the late fifteenth century it was adopted in Rome for use in churches and other buildings associated with the papacy. Later it was taken up by the Holy Roman emperors. Serlio's sixth

---

98 Giles Worsley, *Inigo Jones and the European classicist tradition* (New Haven and London, 2007), 137–55.

23. The Queen's Chapel, St James's Palace, by Inigo Jones (1623–6), east end. Compare with **Figure 53**. (Conway Library, Courtauld Institute of Art, London.)

DESIGN: STAGES AND SOURCES

book of architecture (1547; not published in his lifetime but influential in manuscript form) included numerous Serlianas in designs for royal palaces but only one in a design not associated with royalty. To quote Worsley, 'by the middle of the sixteenth century the Serliana had become a powerful and widely accepted symbol of sovereignty'. How far it retained this symbolic significance, after its introduction into England by Inigo Jones in the early seventeenth century, is perhaps doubtful, for Jones introduced Serlianas into two of his early designs for buildings (not built) that were only peripherally associated with the monarch, and there are other examples in England of its early use in buildings with no royal connection at all (for example, the church of St John, Stanmore of 1630).

However, Jones did include a Serliana in the Queen's Chapel at St James's Palace (built 1623–26), so perhaps some symbolic significance remained. There the Serliana is placed, innovatively, above the altar (Fig. 23), which must surely have served as the model for the Serliana at Pembroke chapel. This, then, is a third point (the others being in the preliminary drawing and the design of the windows) at which Jones's influence can be detected at Pembroke. Worsley suggests that Wren's use of the Serliana here 'resonated across British architecture': such east windows would be used in six of the City churches built under his aegis and in a similar number of the fifty new churches designed by his successors. They were to become commonplace.

We shall see that when Scott came to design his extension to Pembroke chapel he introduced a Serliana much grander than the one Wren had built before him.

Other sources. As we saw in discussing the model, the other chapel windows, three on the north side, four on the south (Figs 24), all follow the same pattern, derived from Inigo Jones's design (see Fig. 8, 25), in which the semi-circular head is surmounted by a straight cornice resting on scroll consoles. These windows are Wren's first use of a design that he made peculiarly his own and which he continued to use throughout his career.[99] By placing a panel below the window it becomes integrated into a unit that stretches from the base of the building almost to the top. The consoles are contained in the width of the stone uprights that lie outside the stone framing of the window itself, so that practical considerations – the form of the

24. A window on the north side. The walls were originally covered with stucco, removed by Scott. (James Austin, c.1993)

25. Inigo Jones's design for the framing of a window, chapel of Somerset House, London (1623). (RIBA Library Drawings and Archives Collections)

---

99 Wren used the same design at St Nicholas, St Edmund, St Magnus and St Anne, Soho among the London churches (Viktor Fürst, *The architecture of Sir Christopher Wren* (London, 1956), 120).

opening for the glazing and the meeting of stonework and surrounding wall – are satisfactorily resolved.

Sekler suggested that the placing of the cupola above the west front (Fig. 19) may have been derived from an engraving in Book III of Cesariano's 1521 edition of Vitruvius.[100] The resemblance is not close, since the cupola shown in the engraving is proportionately much larger than that on the chapel and it is placed centrally over a temple of square plan. The image may in a more general way have suggested a feature crowning the west front. The Pembroke cupola (Fig. 26) is reminiscent of the lanterns commonly featuring in the designs of seventeenth-century English houses: those of Coleshill (1650–62) and Kingston Lacy (1663–65), both by Sir Roger Pratt, are near-contemporary examples.

Dimensions

It was noted above that the height of the side walls of the chapel was increased by about six feet between the preliminary drawing and the model. Two reasons for this may now be suggested.

First, the chapel could obviously not remain as an isolated building and at some point in 1664 (by which time the chapel had been roofed in[101]) the College decided to connect it to Old Court by a cloister with rooms above (Fig. 5). The necessary money was to hand in the form of Sir Robert Hitcham's major bequest, part of which had been used to pay for Hitcham Building. The college now applied to Matthew Wren, as supervisor of Hitcham's will, for leave to use further money from the bequest to build the cloister range.[102] It was obviously desirable that this new range should be of the same height as the existing façade of Old Court along Trumpington Street, which raised the problem of how to handle its abutment to the new chapel. There would have been no difficulty if the new chapel had resembled the old in height and in having a plain front and simple gable (Fig. 2). But this was to be a Classical building and it was important that the cornice of the west front should continue

26. The hexagonal cupola. (James Austin, c.1993)

---

100 Eduard F Sekler, *Wren and his place in European architecture* (London, 1956), 43.
101 Willis and Clark, vol. 1, 147. There appears to be no document in the College Archives that actually records this date, but it is a reasonable assumption, given that the contract for the carpentry was signed early in January 1665.
102 Ibid.

uninterrupted around the sides of the building. The side walls therefore had to be made high enough to allow the cornice to clear the ridge of the cloister range. (Today the ridge of the cloister intrudes into the chapel cornice by about six inches but this was almost certainly not the case originally, for when Scott extended the chapel he also made considerable alterations to the range of buildings along Trumpington Street, which necessitated raising their roofline.[103]) That the necessary height of the chapel was already provided for in the model suggests strongly that the cloister range had been envisaged by this stage, even though the round window over the door in the model still implies a free-standing building. Perhaps Wren foresaw that the chapel would one day be integrated into the existing college but did not wish to seem to pre-judge the issue.

The second reason for the increase in height is probably more important. Given that Wren's west front adhered to the square proportions of Serlio's temple-front design, the height would determine the width of the building. Were the cornice to have been kept as low as in the preliminary drawing, the chapel interior would have been both low and narrow. Indeed, Wren's initial strategy might have been to decide on an optimum width for the building and allow that to determine the height.

Conveniently, these two considerations pointed in the same direction, which would no doubt have pleased Christopher Wren. The increased height also contributes importantly to the striking presence of the chapel as seen from the street, which would presumably have pleased his uncle.

With regard to other proportions, the simple ratios found in the preliminary drawing are much less pervasive but can still be found. For example, the overall length of the building is twice its height (measured to the top of the cornice); the width of the windows is related to the distance between them in the ratio 4:3; the pilasters are ten times as high as wide (as were the pilaster strips of the preliminary drawing) and the central (brick) area of the panels below the side and west windows is a square. The interior length of the chapel (excluding the ante-chapel) is twice the width. Figure 27 illustrates some rather more interesting mathematical features of the west front. The whole façade is contained in a rectangle of the proportions 4:3, but here Wren appears to have used geometry rather than simple ratios as an ordering principle, lines connecting principal points defining the position of other or subsidiary features. For example, the major diagonals of the rectangle (*ad*), intersect precisely at the centre point of the round-headed top of the window – this point being the centre of the whole façade. The lines *bd* pass through the centre of the inner pilasters. The central point of the top of

---

103 Letter of Sir George Gabriel Stokes (acting Master of Pembroke) to Scott, 18 May 1880, giving the College's agreement 'That the roof of the west side of First Court should be raised a little' (RIBA Collection, SC/CA/PC/305).

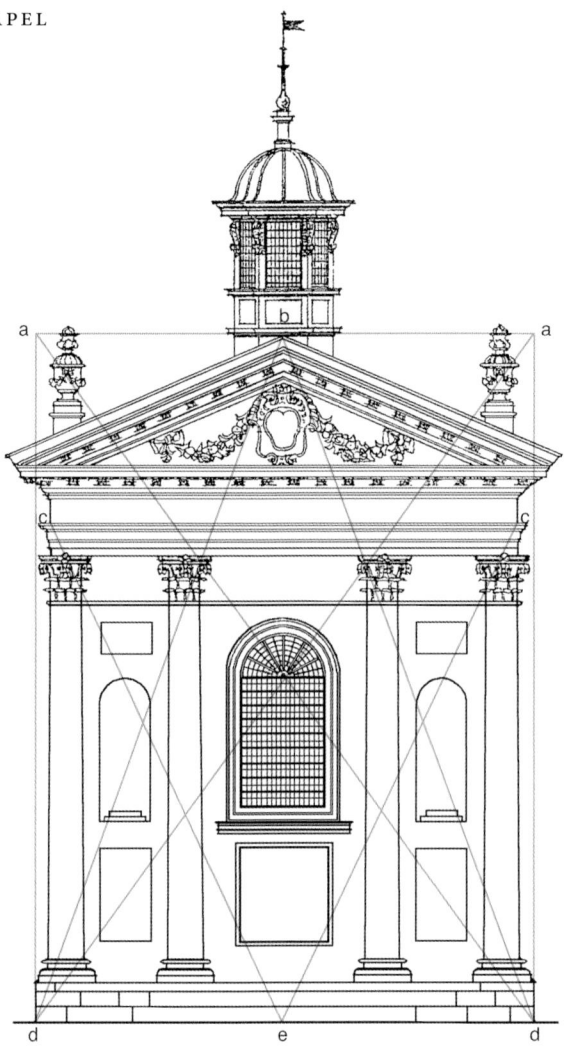

27. The geometry of the west front. In a rectangle *aadd*, drawn to enclose the elevation, the diagonals *ad* intersect exactly at the centre of the semicircular top of the window. The lines *bd* cross the centre of the pilasters at the bottom of their capitals, and the lines *ce* cross the centre of the side recesses.

the round-headed niches is defined by *ce*.[104] It should not, of course, surprise us that, in designing his earliest building, a mathematician should turn to geometry for help. 'Geometrical Figures', he wrote, 'are naturally more beautiful than other irregular; in this all consent as to a Law of Nature. Of geometrical figures, the Square and the Circle are most beautiful'.[105]

A minor, unrelated point concerning the dimensions of the chapel may be noted here. The west front is placed slightly obliquely with respect to the east–west axis, so that the north side is about fifteen inches longer than the south. The difference is taken up entirely at the west end of the ante-chapel (Fig. 4). As he was to do later in several of the City churches, Wren was here adapting to an irregular site, arising from a slight change in direction of Trumpington Street.

104 For some related constructions see Sekler, *Wren*, 81 and Figs 13–16.
105 Wren, *Parentalia*, 351. For a discussion of Wren's mathematical thinking in relation to architecture see Soo, *Wren's 'tracts'*, 202.

THE VAULT

As the resting place of the donor, the vault is perhaps an appropriate place to begin the description of the chapel as built. As it happens, it also sheds some light on the men who worked on the building.

The vault runs north–south across the full width of the chapel, passing immediately below where the altar originally was (Fig. 28a). It has a shallow barrel vault with a maximum height of about 1.7 metres (Fig. 28d). The ceiling is brought as close as possible to the overlying chapel floor. The walls and ceiling are rendered; the floor is of brick. Access is gained now only from outside the chapel, by lifting a stone slab adjacent to the north wall, which discourages frequent entry (but see pp. 110–11). [106]

As Matthew Wren's will seems to imply (p.12), it had been foreseen that it would be difficult to keep the vault dry. Perhaps this was especially the case because of the tributary of Hobson's Conduit, noted above (p.31), which might well have leaked. Raising the floor of the chapel at the east end, as Matthew Wren suggested allowed the floor of the underlying vault to be brought higher and there are in fact three steps up to the east end. A document in the College Archives, however, shows that water was seeping in even as building was going on and suggestions are made about how to deal with this.[107] These include 'extra strong brickwork', raising the level of the chapel floor by another step and even the sinking of a well at the north-east corner of the building. Seepage was certainly a problem a century later, when an interment in the vault took place, though this may have been caused by eighteenth-century garden water-works, which included a pond close to the east end of the chapel.[108] However, there is no mention of water when the vault was entered in 1879, at the time of Scott's work, and when the vault was inspected in 1999 it was dry.

The vault is almost entirely filled with nine massive stone sarcophagi (Fig. 28b, c; Fig. 29) oriented east–west, closely spaced and arranged in chronological order of the death of their occupants, starting with Matthew Wren at the south end. All are raised on brick or stone supports, possibly to help keep

---

[106] A description and sketch plans of the vault are given in a letter of 17 November 1879 from George Kett (builder) to G G Scott (RIBA Collection, SC/CA/PC/231). The vault was accurately surveyed and photographed for the first time in 1999 (A V Grimstone, 'The vault under the college chapel', *PAG*, 74 (2000), 33–36).

[107] PCA, Hardwick F3.

[108] This was the burial of Roger Long (Master) in 1770 (Attwater, *Pembroke College*, 100).

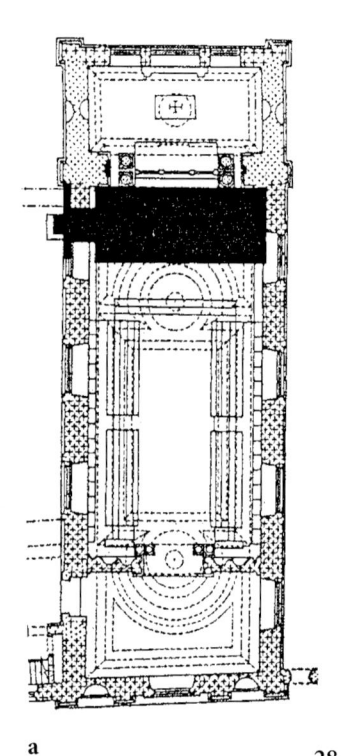

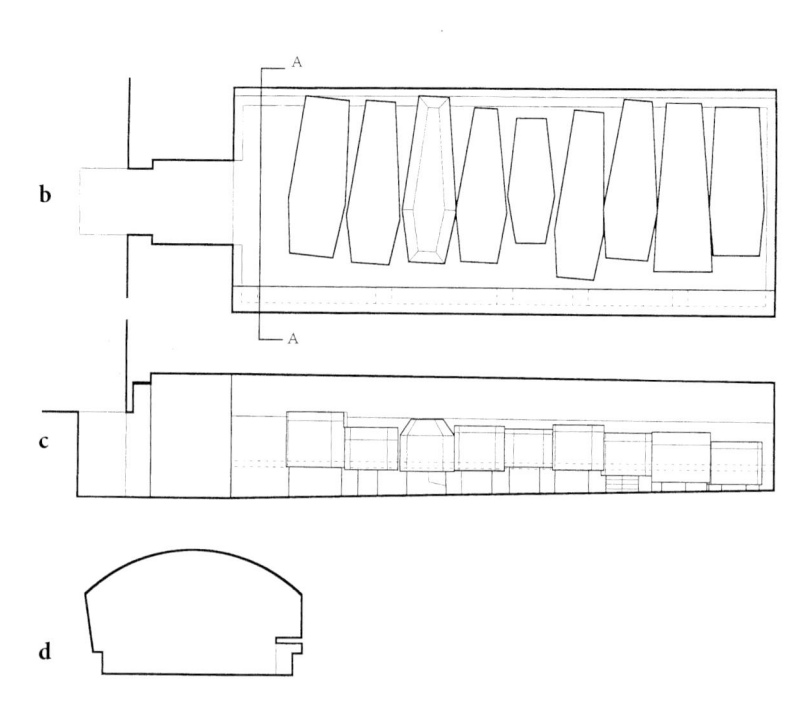

28. The vault. (a) Location plan, showing the vault (black) extending north-south across the chapel, below where the altar originally stood. (b) Plan, with most of the space occupied by the nine sarcophagi. That of Matthew Wren, the first to be entombed here, is at the south end, furthest from the entrance. (c) Longitudinal and (d) cross sections, the latter showing the shallow barrel vault. (Survey and drawings by James Campbell, 1999.)

them above water. They may have been shifted into their present very regular arrangement as part of Scott's work. Matthew Wren's body was enclosed according to his instructions in a lead inner coffin and there was no doubt something similar in the others. It has been suggested that 'such a comprehensive encapsulation of encoffined remains within stone sarcophagi as . . . at Pembroke is unique in England'.[109] Those interred, apart from Matthew Wren, are two of his sons, Matthew and Charles, the latter's son, Thomas, and five Masters of the College.[110] From the size of his sarcophagus, it is evident that Matthew Wren was a small man, not much above five feet tall, much like his nephew.

Numerous graffiti, in the form of initials or names, are present in the vault, mostly in two groups, on the south end wall and on the wall and ceiling adjacent to the entrance. It is clear that these initials were incised into the

---

109 Julian W S Litten, personal communication, 31 December 1999.
110 Further details are given in Appendix 1.

29. The vault, looking south.
(Ian Fleming, 2007)

rendering before it hardened. The date '1664' commonly occurs among them. These initials are likely to be those of builders and craftsmen working on the earlier stages of construction of the chapel (bricklayers, masons and carpenters). 'Robert G(r?). . .' probably denotes Robert Grumbold, the likely mason contractor (see p. 63), and 'RB' and 'WB' could well be Richard and William Billopps, who appear as craftsmen in the contract for the woodwork (see p. 79).[111] 'WS 1665' is probably William Sampson, fellow and Treasurer at the time and a witness of the same contract. Most of these initials, however, are enigmatic.

The date '1665' also appears more than once and is more likely to apply to craftsmen working on the chapel interior.[112] Among these, and of particular importance, is a carefully inscribed 'E P 1665' (Fig. 30). The vault was

111 Other names and initials that can be read with reasonable certainty are: EGAA, RA, WB 1674, WC, John Danks, RF, FALD (or IALD?), Gardiner, IH, RK, TK 1665, F (or J) M, John NASH, DP 1665, R/R, ROWLES, GW, RoWI, SW.
112 The dates '1666' and '1672' also appear, once each.

30. The inscription 'EP 1665' on the ceiling of the vault. (Ian Fleming, 2007)

presumably plastered only once, so that in 1665 inscriptions could not be incised into wet rendering. Instead, the 'E P 1665' is formed of rows of closely set small holes, probably made with a fine punch and a mallet. This is the clearest, most painstakingly cut of all the inscriptions and stands apart from the others, on the ceiling of the vault, suggesting that whoever made it felt entitled to assert a degree of importance. Given the identification of Edward Pearce as the draughtsman responsible for the preliminary drawing, these initials may reasonably be taken to be his. However, 1665 is something like three years later than the date of the drawing. Would Pearce have come to Pembroke at that late date and painstakingly inscribed his initials in the vault simply to mark his early work on the chapel design? The date surely suggests that that he was working on the chapel in some other capacity, in the later stages of construction. Evidence for this will be presented later.

These initials are important because, apart from the names of the carpenters and bricklayers, the College's archives disclose almost nothing about the craftsmen who worked on the chapel. Records of payments to them were probably kept separately from the main college accounts and the total was added up only when the chapel was finished, so that a bill could be sent to Matthew Wren. Subsequently, these records of individual payments probably seemed unimportant and were discarded.[113]

113 During the building of the Wren Library at Trinity College, payments to builders were recorded in a notebook, probably by the master mason, Robert Grumbold, who also acted as clerk of the works (see Howard Colvin, 'The Building', in David McKitterick (ed.), *The making of the Wren Library, Trinity College,* Cambridge (Cambridge, 1995) 39–40).

THE EXTERIOR

The model shows in some detail what the external form of the chapel was to be. How was it translated into brick and stone?

Brickwork: the side elevations

A contract (in the College Archives) for the brickwork of the chapel, throws interesting light on what were presumably Wren's original intentions (though there is no mention of him in the document) for the treatment of the side elevations.[114] The contract was signed three days after the foundation stone of the chapel had been laid by the Master, Mark Franck, in the name of Bishop Wren, on 13 May 1663.[115] The contract reads:

> May 16, 1663.
> Articles of Agreement made between the R^t Wor^l Master Franck D^r in Divinity M^r of P. Hall, and E. Stearne one of the Fellowes of the sayd Coll on the one part; And George Jackson and Tho. Hutton of Cambridge Bricklayers on the other part, Concerning the Brick-work of a new Chapell to be built at the Coll. aforesayd as followeth.
>
> It is Covenanted and agreed between the parties abovesayd, That the walls of the Chapell above the second Plint up to the Roofe shall contain in thicknes fower bricks in length; and that the Heads and sides of all the Bricks wch shall appear outwards shall be all ground, and fine ioynts made.
>
> That the work under the windowes shall be sett out 2 or 3 Inches to the thicknes of the second Plint, and so ordered that the Bricks shall rise in the midst after the forme of Stonework if the Modell so require it.[116]
>
> That for this work the sayd Dr F. or Mr S. shall pay unto the sayd G. Jackson and Tho. Hutton, fower pounds, fifteen shillings per pole for every pole of square measure, the windowes not reckoned to make up the measure. They

---

114 The original document cannot at present be located. The transcription follows that in *Wren Society*, vol. 5, 27–8, which differs in minor respects from that in Willis and Clark, vol. 1, 155.
115 Wren, *Parentalia*, 52.
116 As noted previously, the term 'model' could refer at this time to both a drawing and a three-dimensional model. Since a wooden model certainly existed at Pembroke, it seems to be this to which the contract refers, particularly as the contract for the woodwork (see below) refers not to a 'model' but to 'a certaine forme and draught of Joyners work'.

the sayd Jackson and Hutton being at all charges of workmanshipp except the laying their materialls by them.

That the Foundation work up to the second plint shall be reckoned at the same rate.

That the Brickwork the outside whereof shall be covered with Ashlaer shall be accounted for as inward work, at the Rate of 30^s per pole for a Brick and half thick proportionably.

The chapel walls as built are approximately three feet thick, agreeing with the 'four bricks in length' of the contract. The contract gives no details of their construction but inspection from within the roof-space shows that the cavity between the inner and outer skins of brick is filled with rubble.

The document gives rates for brickwork per square pole[117] and they are rates only for laying the bricks, not for providing them. The College would presumably have entered into a contract with another party for supplying the bricks. The phrase 'if the Modell so require it' suggests that the model was not yet to hand when the contract was signed and that important points of the design were still to be settled. Given Matthew Wren's age, the College would have wanted to proceed with building as quickly as possible and was therefore securing bricklayers in advance at piece rates, rather than being able to negotiate a price for the whole job. Yet in referring in some detail to 'the work under the windowes' the contract implies that here at least the design must have been well advanced and was known to the College, perhaps through drawings.

The contract's provision that the brickwork under the windows should be 'sett out 2 or 3 Inches to the thicknes of the second Plint' (and therefore project above the general level of the wall),[118] and that it 'shall rise in the midst after the forme of Stonework', can be readily related to the stone-framed panels below the side windows, which are represented in the model (Fig. 13) and present in the chapel as built (Fig. 5). There are panels below the windows of the east and west façades but these were surely conceived as being faced with stone from the outset. We can be reasonably sure that at least in the panels below the side windows the bricks were originally intended to be 'appearing outwards' and were therefore what would now be called facing bricks.[119] The contract does not allow us to deduce what was intended for the rest of the side walls: it could also have been brickwork or it could have been ashlar, in which case the slightly projecting panels below the windows, of facing bricks framed

117 A pole is sixteen feet.
118 The first plinth is presumably the termination of the foundation brickwork, now below ground level.
119 That is, bricks cut accurately to size and laid with fine joints made with putty rather than mortar. See *Wren Society*, vol. 5, 27 n. 2 and J W P Campbell and A Saint, 'The manufacture and dating of English brickwork, 1600–1720', *Archaeological Journal*, 159 (2002), 170–93.

by stone, would have contrasted with an otherwise ashlared wall surface. The resulting changes in depth, material and colour across the wall would have given an interesting articulation to the façade. In the event – except for the stonework of the plinth, the framing of the windows and the framing of the panels below them – the side walls, including the middle of the panels, were built entirely of common (that is, not facing) bricks, which were covered with stucco. There was no exposed brickwork at all. We know this because, when Scott removed the stucco in 1880, no bricks 'all ground, and fine ioynts made' were to be seen.[120] One can only speculate what caused this change of plan. Perhaps it was done more for speed than economy. However, Wren's one surviving drawing for Emmanuel College chapel, dated 1666, shows the ranges on either side of the chapel faced with brick, but by 1669 this intention was abandoned in favour of limestone ashlar, perhaps (Stubbings suggests) because the success of the Dutch fleet in impeding the Newcastle colliers had so inflated the price of coal that bricks cost more than stone.[121]

The west and east façades

There is nothing in the contract for the brickwork that specifically refers to the east and west façades. As suggested, they were probably always intended to be ashlared, the stone being laid over common bricks. Both of these façades are covered wholly with stone: Portland for the plinths, Ketton for the remainder. The design of these façades has already been discussed and illustrated in the account of the chapel model and the sources of the design. On the whole, what was built is close to what is shown in the model, though occasional differences show refinement of the design in progress.

The design of the west façade, with its sunk panel below the window and the round-headed niches with sunk panels above and below, is carried through from model to building almost without change. In his later buildings, Wren would use such sunk panels repeatedly as a way of articulating an area of blank wall. The one part of this façade that Wren had to devise was the window, for none was present in Serlio's engraving, which he otherwise followed meticulously. For its dimensions and overall shape he simply repeated the pattern of the side windows, but he departed from this (and from Inigo Jones and Edward Pearce) by giving the west window a plain stone frame, without a keystone or the other embellishments of cornice and brackets. The difference in the treatment can just be seen in Fig. 19, which provides the only possible simultaneous view of the west front and a side

---

120 Signs of the stucco can still be seen on the sides of some of the stonework below the windows, where the profile of the inner inch or so (originally covered by stucco) is sharp and unworn while the outer inch has been eroded by weathering.
121 Stubbings, *Emmanuel College chapel*, 8–9 and pl. 6; Geraghty, *Architectural drawings*, 24, no. 8; AS I, 100.

elevation of the chapel; the difference would be more evident (and probably more disconcerting) if one could walk around the building and have these two elevations in clear view at once.

For the central light of the east façade, Wren wanted a somewhat wider window than those of the side elevations and perhaps sought some logical basis for its width. He achieved this by taking advantage of the fact that the reveals of all the other windows are splayed, and he therefore adopted for the east window not the external width of the other windows but the width of their opening presented to the interior. The framing of all the windows of the east façade is kept very simple. In both model and chapel, the divisions between the central and lateral lights are of plain masonry: there are no columns or pilasters (Fig. 22).

Indeed, the whole east façade has a plainness of treatment that seems at odds with the richness of the west front. They might almost come from two different buildings, and the side elevations from a third. As others have pointed out, either from inexperience or from working in haste, Wren seems to have designed separate elevations but not to have brought together the exterior of his building as a whole. A weakness in a point of Classical detail on the chapel exterior may similarly reveal the novice architect, or his failure to exert adequate control of his builders: a footnote in one of the *Wren Society* volumes sternly points out that 'The extraordinary error by which the architect does not keep the face of the pilasters on the façade does not exist in the model.'[122] The fault referred to is that the outer edges of the pilasters project beyond the sides of the façade, and beyond the edges of the architrave and frieze above (Fig. 19). The face of the frieze should normally align with the face of the pilaster. The error may have arisen from the late decision not to ashlar the sides of the building.

Decorative panels are used on the east façade below the Serliana and above its two side windows, but here there are differences between the model and the building, allowing us to see Wren refining his design. In the model the panels above the two side windows are shown as being simply rectangles of stonework raised slightly *above* the level of the surrounding wall (Fig. 13). In the building, however, these become sunk panels, like those of the west façade (Fig. 19). A panel extends below the full width of the Serliana and here something a little more complex was evidently thought necessary. In the model, this whole area is raised slightly above the level of the surrounding wall surface and its central region is raised still further. In the chapel, the area below the Serliana takes the more definite form of a fielded panel, with the border now a broad, shallow frame around a central area of raised stonework (Fig. 22).

---

122 *Wren Society*, vol. 5, 27 n. 2.

The stone entablature of the west and east fronts continues round the building but on the side elevations the frieze (the middle element) is a plain band of brick; timber was originally used for the block cornice above.[123]

The master mason for the chapel, as already intimated, was probably Robert Grumbold. He had recently worked at Pembroke in Ivy Court and what is probably his name occurs in the vault (see p. 57). Born in 1639 and living in Cambridge, he was one of a noted family of masons. He would have been only twenty-three or twenty-four years old when work on the chapel began, but his reputation must already have been growing, for in 1667 he was paid by the Deans and Canons of Worcester for a journey from Cambridge to survey the cathedral. He subsequently worked closely with Wren on Emmanuel College chapel,[124] and later, as the leading master-builder in Cambridge, he was to oversee the building of the Wren library at Trinity College, Cambridge (begun in 1676), for which work he received a guinea a week. He it was (the 'honest and skilfull artificer' in Hawksmoor's phrase) who went up to London to consult Wren when necessary.[125] He would have been the obvious choice as mason contractor for Pembroke chapel and may have had a similar supervisory role over the building work. As mason he would have been responsible for the general stonework of the east and west ends and, on the side elevations, for the stonework around and below the windows, and the plinth and cornice. Grumbold was also capable of doing the less demanding kind of stone carving. The ribbons and flowers on the keystones of the windows (Fig. 24) and the scrolls and small flowers on the sides of the consoles supporting the cornices above them (Fig. 19) are less free in style than the other carving and might well be his work. There is, however, nothing to suggest that he was responsible for the major decorative stone carving of the exterior, now to be considered.

Stone carving

Here we are dealing principally with the urns on the corners of the roof, the cartouche and festoons in the west pediment and the Corinthian capitals of the west and east fronts. The stone cross surmounting the east end (Fig. 22) has been described as nineteenth-century and its good state of preservation suggests that this may be so.[126] However, it is shown in identical form in Scott's survey drawing of the original chapel, so that, if he replaced it, he followed the original pattern.[127]

---

123 During restoration in 1970 concrete modillions were substituted for oak.
124 Stubbings, *Emmanuel College chapel*, 10–11.
125 Colvin 'The Building', 39–40. See also Colvin, *Biographical dictionary*, 454–5, for a resumé of Grumbold's career as designer and builder in Cambridge.
126 RCHM, *Cambridge*, part 2, 153.
127 Scott drawing, SCGGJ[13]87 in RIBA Collection.

Wall drawings for stone carving. In 1964, during restoration work in Hitcham Building, two remarkable wall drawings came to light in a room on the first floor (now called the Thomas Gray Room). This must have been unfinished when the chapel was under construction: panelling was not yet in place and the drawings were made on the plastered walls. The room may have been used as an office or workroom by the builders, or perhaps it simply provided some conveniently bare walls to make large-scale drawings on, which would later be covered up.

One of the drawings, on the south wall of the room, is of a flaming urn (Fig. 31); the other, on the east wall, is of the cartouche and one of the festoons in the west pediment (Fig. 38). Both are drawn at full scale. Done in black chalk, they are in some respects detailed and highly finished, in other respects freely drawn; they appear to be the work of the same, competent draughtsman.[128] They can be added to the preliminary drawing, the chapel model and the pilaster base drawings as a fourth, precious contribution to the meagre stock of visual materials relating to the chapel's design.

Like the model, the drawings probably had more than one function. They would have served to show Wren (assuming he saw them) and the fellows of the College what was being proposed for these carvings: they are large enough, and the room is large enough, for the viewer to be able to stand back and take in their effect. Both drawings place the carvings in context: for the cartouche and festoon there is a sloping line indicating the upper margin of the pediment; for the urn, its plinth and the roof-line below are carefully outlined. The drawings could also represent a late stage in the evolution of the design of these structures.

Arnold Pacey, who studied the drawings in some detail, noted the presence on both drawings of construction lines: on the urn, for example, there is a vertical line on the central axis and indications of compass-drawn curves, perhaps defining the shape of the urn's bowl and its proportions – lines probably used in setting out the drawing.[129] They could also have been transferred to a block of stone, raising the possibility that the drawings might have been intended as working drawings for the stone carver. Pacey suggests that the drawings might be seen as a survival of a medieval tradition of making full-size drawings of decorative or structural details, often on walls or floors, as a stage in the production of the templates to be used by the masons or carvers. Such templates were obviously important in ensuring uniformity in repetitive work and Pacey suggests that such templates would have been needed at Pembroke, to ensure that the four urns were identical.

---

128 A third drawing, on the west wall, in black and red chalk and showing the head and shoulders of a bearded man in Jacobean dress, is seemingly unrelated to the chapel and is much inferior in quality to the other drawings. It is difficult to believe that it could be from the same hand.

129 Arnold Pacey, *Medieval architectural drawing* (Stroud, 2007), 213–18.

THE EXTERIOR

This, however, is conjectural. All one can safely say is that the drawings represent a late but not final stage in the thoughts of the designer, for we shall see that the urn drawing differs significantly from what was eventually carved.

As to the designer, Denys Spittle wrote of the drawings that 'it would be tempting to attribute them to someone in Wren's circle for the guidance of a local mason'.[130] At this stage, however, Wren did not have such a circle. It will be argued that it is more likely that designer and carver were the same man and that he can probably be identified.

31. Wall drawing of an urn, attributed to Edward Pearce. The drapery is drawn explicitly as a lambrequin: that is, with a decorated border (*cf.* Figs. 36 and 68.) The swags run continuously around the urn, without the intervening masks of the final design. (Ian Fleming, 2008)

The urns. The flaming urns on the four corners of the chapel can be seen as replacing the pineapple or pine-cone finials of the preliminary drawing, an appropriate substitution given the funereal intent of the building. The exposed position of the urns led to their more rapid erosion than the rest of the decorative carving and at some point, very probably as part of Scott's work on the chapel in 1880, the flames and covers of the urns were renewed (Fig. 32). By 1970, complete replacement was necessary (Fig. 33). Enough of the carving survived at that time to allow the original form of the urns to be reproduced.[131] In most respects the urns thus modelled closely resemble what is shown in the wall drawing. The overall shape, the swags of

130 Denys Spittle, 'Wall-paintings at Pembroke College, Cambridge', *Transactions of the Ancient Monuments Society*, 16 (1969), 109–114.
131 The drawing for the new urns was made by Denys Spittle. One of the old urns, badly weathered, is now in the Fellows' Garden at Pembroke, and other fragments are at the west end of Library Lawn.

THE SEVENTEENTH-CENTURY CHAPEL

32. Urn, photographed in 1970. The gadrooned cover and the flames were probably renewed by Scott. On the lower part of the urn, not renewed, traces of the masks and drapery swags are visible. The swags do not run directly from mask to mask, but are looped up at intermediate points between them, as in the wall drawing (and as in Fig. 33). (Pembroke College Architectural Archive.)

33. Replacement urn of 1970, carved according to a reconstruction by Denys Spittle. (Pembroke College Architectural Archive.)

34. Urn from Loggan's engraving of Pembroke College (Fig. 2, detail).

drapery, the gadrooned cover with its narrow mouth from which the flames emerge: all are the same. The flames themselves are similar in outline but cannot match three-dimensionally in stone the realism and freedom with which they are drawn. There is one major difference, however, between carving and drawing: four heads (or masks) have now appeared on each urn, gripping in their mouths the swags of drapery that run round the bowl and linking them together. These heads are depicted in Loggan's engraving, confirming that they formed part of the original urns (Fig. 34). There are no such heads in the drawing, in which the swags of drapery run continuously around the urn. Second thoughts obviously prevailed even at the stage of the full-size drawing. As with the brickwork, there was apparently a late change of plan.

The drawing shows details of the drapery which were entirely eroded on the urns. Curling ribbons knot the ends of the swags; we shall come across similar ribbons again later. In the swags themselves an important detail must be noted: the lower edge of the drapery is scalloped. This same emphasis of the edge is seen in the folds of drapery hanging down from the end of each swag. This feature characterises a decorative motif called a lambrequin. The word originally denoted the scarf draped across a knight's helmet, which came to be represented in stylised form in heraldry. Later, it was applied to any fringe-like border carved on furniture or painted on ceramics. In the form shown in the urn drawing it appears repeatedly in sixteenth- and seventeenth-century Continental engravings of decorative designs.[132] Simple swags or folds of drapery with plain borders are common enough in English decorative work of the seventeenth century (for example, in Grinling Gibbons' carving) but drapery with the scalloped or otherwise decorated border of the lambrequin is to be distinguished from this. It is a motif found repeatedly in the work of both the elder and the younger Edward Pearce and we shall find another example of it in Pembroke chapel (see p. 101).

A close parallel to the Pembroke urns and to the wall drawing exists elsewhere in Cambridge. Figure 35 shows one of the urns on the gate piers at the entrance to Clare College. The urn itself is strongly reminiscent, stylistically and in its proportions, of those at Pembroke. There are the same swags of drapery, gripped here in the mouths of lion masks, and with lambrequins as in the Pembroke drawing. The Clare urns are known to be the work of the younger Edward Pearce, to whom payment for 'carving about the gates' was made in 1675.[133] They are surmounted by fruit and flowers rather than flames. Pearce carved similar baskets of flowers (in wood) on the newel posts of the staircase at Sudbury Hall, Derbyshire, in 1676.[134] In the absence of documentary evidence the Pembroke urns cannot certainly be attributed to him, but the similarities to his work at Clare are striking. Pearce carved other urns during his career: his monument to Margaret Vernon in All Saints church at Sudbury (also of 1676) is surmounted by a large flaming urn with gadrooned cover; at St Andrews, Holborn, he was paid £10 for '4 Urnes each 3 ft. high, 50s. per peece'[135] and (on a grander scale)

35. Urn on a gate pier at Clare College, Cambridge, carved by Edward Pearce. The lambrequin drapery swags are gripped in the mouths of lion masks.
(Ian Fleming, 2007)

---

132 I am much indebted to Tim Newbery for instruction about the lambrequin. For sixteenth-century examples see the engravings by René Boyvin, Cornelius Bos and others in Rudolf Berliner, *Ornamentale Vorlageblätter des 15 bis 18 Jahrhunderts* (Leipzig, 1925), vol. 2.
133 Willis and Clark, vol. 1, 104. The gate piers themselves were built by Robert Grumbold in 1673 (ibid.).
134 Beard and Knott, 'Edward Pearce's work at Sudbury'.
135 *Wren Society*, vol. 10, 103.

36. Urn, in an engraving by Edward Pearce senior (1647). Drapery swags are looped up between human or animal masks, as in Figures 33 and 35. (Rijksmuseum, Amsterdam.)

he carved urns for the gardens at Hampton Court.[136] If he carved them, he would almost certainly have designed them as well. Pearce's drawings for wall monuments frequently include urns, often with gadrooned covers and flames,[137] which may account for Pacey's significant observation that, in the urn drawing, the flames suggest the work of someone used to working in relief rather than in the round. The draughtsmanship in Pearce's drawings is usually freer than that of the wall drawing but this is to be expected if the latter was intended as a working drawing for the carver. There is nothing in the wall drawing to suggest that Pearce could not be responsible for it. If the attribution of the Pembroke wall drawings to Pearce is correct they would be unique examples of his drawings at full scale.

In the light of this supposition it is perhaps possible to trace the design of the urns a stage further back. Pearce's father, perhaps primarily a painter, was also skilled in decorative design. In 1640 he made a set of engravings of carved ornament, the so-called *Book of friezes*, which will be discussed later in relation to the chapel wood-carving. He also produced a second suite of engravings of grotesque ornament, dated 1647, the only known complete copy of which, in Berlin, was destroyed at the end of the Second World War.[138] However, two of the engravings from this set were reproduced by Berliner[139]

---

136 Kerry Downes, *English Baroque architecture* (London, 1966), pl. 73, and *Wren Society*, vol. 17, plate 7.
137 For example, in his design for a monument to Viscount Irwin (Soane Collection, 61) and a monument for an unidentified subject, also in the Soane Collection (62).
138 Simon Jervis, 'A seventeenth-century book of engraved ornament', *Burlington Magazine*, 128 (1986), 893–903.
139 Berliner, *Ornamentale Vorlageblätter*, vol. 3, pl. 279.

THE EXTERIOR

37. Carving in the west pediment. Note that it fits tightly into the available space. (Ian Fleming, 2009)

38. Wall drawing for the carving in the west pediment, attributed to Edward Pearce. This is very close to the carving. The guide-line indicating the top edge of the pediment suggests that the drawing was made after the pediment had been designed.

and these, together with two others, survive in the Rijksmuseum.[140] One of them (Fig. 36) shows an urn close in style to those at Pembroke and Clare. Crowned with a basket of fruit and foliage, it is decorated with both festoons of fruit and flowers and swags of drapery, the latter attached to masks – of which there would have been four, just as in the Pembroke urns. The whole urn, it may be noted, is backed by an outspread lambrequin with scalloped border.

All things considered, it seems reasonable to take the urns as a second manifestation of Edward Pearce's connection with Pembroke chapel, this time as a designer and carver in stone. Arnold Pacey first raised the possibility that this might be the case in an unpublished typescript of 2002 but was unable to carry his investigation further.

West pediment. The carving here consists of a large central cartouche bordered by bold scroll-work and flanked by festoons of fruit and flowers, tied with bows at each end, all finely rendered (Fig. 37). The related wall drawing (Fig. 38) is very close to the actual carving. In both the carving fills the space in the pediment.

140 A V Griffiths, '"The print in Stuart Britain" revisited', *Print Quarterly*, 17 (2000), 118.

69

The same general design of a central cartouche with flanking festoons was used by Wren at Emmanuel College chapel, though seemingly not in his later work. Its origins are probably French and can be found, for example, in the Sorbonne chapel of 1635, designed by Lemercier and known in England from prints in the early 1660s. Hugh May used the same design at Eltham Lodge, built in 1663–64 and contemporary with Pembroke chapel. The pediment carving at Pembroke is well preserved and of high quality. The swelling, rounded forms of the cartouche, both in the central boss and the scrolls surrounding it, coupled with the deep undercutting, are perhaps the first manifestation in Pembroke chapel of the auricular decorative style that will be found more obviously used in the interior (see p. 86). The festoons, with their close-packed fruit, are reminiscent of those in the elder Pearce's *Book of friezes* (Fig. 48), to be discussed later.

If the Pembroke urns are accepted as the work of Edward Pearce, it would be reasonable – given the stylistic similarity of the two wall drawings – to suggest that the carving in the west pediment is also his. Much later, Pearce used the same general design in pediments at Combe Abbey (1682–83) and the Bishop's Palace at Lichfield (1686–87).[141] There are stylistic differences between his pediment carvings at those two buildings and that at Pembroke, possibly attributable to the gap of twenty years and Pearce's openness to new styles (see pp. 117–118).

Pilaster capitals. The finely carved Corinthian capitals of the pilasters on the east and west ends of the chapel (Fig. 59) were noted by Kerry Downes as being of an unusual type, but without further explanation.[142] Their most distinctive feature is that the caulicole (the upwardly springing vine shoots from which the spiral volutes arise) are treated with more than usual emphasis, standing out prominently from the surrounding foliage and with their upper parts (from which the volutes arise) supported on long thin stalks with swelling caps. No related designs for the Pembroke capitals are known, but a drawing of a Corinthian capital for St Paul's cathedral by Edward Pearce (Fig. 60) is generally similar and gives the same emphasis to the caulicole. The chapel capitals are most likely to have been designed and carved by whoever was responsible for the other important decorative stone carving, and a reasonable conclusion is that this was Pearce – a suggestion that will receive further support when the capitals of the reredos are brought into the picture (pp. 94–6).

---

141 H M Colvin, 'Letters and papers relating to the rebuilding of Combe Abbey, Warwickshire, 1681–1686', *Walpole Society*, 50 (1984), 248–309; H M Colvin and A Oswald, 'The bishop's palace, Lichfield', *Country Life*, 116 (30 December 1954), 2312–15.
142 Downes, *Architecture of Wren*, 122, n. 80.

THE INTERIOR

Wren had designed a box, roofed some time in 1664.[143] How was the interior to be planned and brought into being? Wren's grasp of structural problems and his study of antique temples and Classical detail would have been less relevant at this point.

The ante-chapel and organ loft

At the west end of the building the final bay forms the spacious ante-chapel (Fig. 4), with the organ loft above. Chapel and ante-chapel are separated by a wooden screen, vertical timbers within which carry part of the weight of the loft. The ante-chapel is panelled throughout. Coupled wooden columns with Corinthian capitals frame the entrance to the main body of the chapel (Figs 4, 39, 80) There is a single step up from the ante-chapel to chapel.

Kerry Downes conjectured that, because the division between the body of the chapel and the ante-chapel and organ loft is not marked by a corresponding division in the ceiling (as it is in Emmanuel College chapel), the loft must be an afterthought.[144] However, the contract for the woodwork, to be discussed shortly (pp. 79–81), refers to both the organ loft and the 'outer chapell' (that is, the ante-chapel). Furthermore, there was an organ in the old chapel and every reason to think that the College would have wanted the new chapel to be similarly equipped.[145] The fact that the ceiling design does not reflect the ante-chapel below might indicate haste in planning but in practice does not appear as a weakness.

An unexpected feature of the organ loft came to light during repairs in 1979 when removal of the flooring revealed the timber framing for an oculus, some six feet in diameter and with evidence of a surrounding balustrade (Fig. 40). This would have allowed light from the large west window to penetrate into the ante-chapel. The present transition from the dark ante-chapel to the

---

143 Willis and Clark, vol. 1, 147.
144 Downes, *Architecture of Wren*, 31.
145 The organ originally placed in the loft is believed to be that from the old chapel, its case probably dating from the 1630s and therefore surviving Dowsing's visitation. This organ was re-built by Thomas Thamar in 1674, and in 1708 it was moved to Framlingham church, Suffolk, where it remains. The present organ (Fig. 39), dating from 1708–10 and built by Charles Quarles, was extensively enlarged in the nineteenth and twentieth centuries, and restored to a near approximation of its original state in 1980. (See articles in *PAG*, 45 (1971), 17–19 (by 'M.G.'), and 55 (1981), 14–18 (by Sidney Kenderdine).)

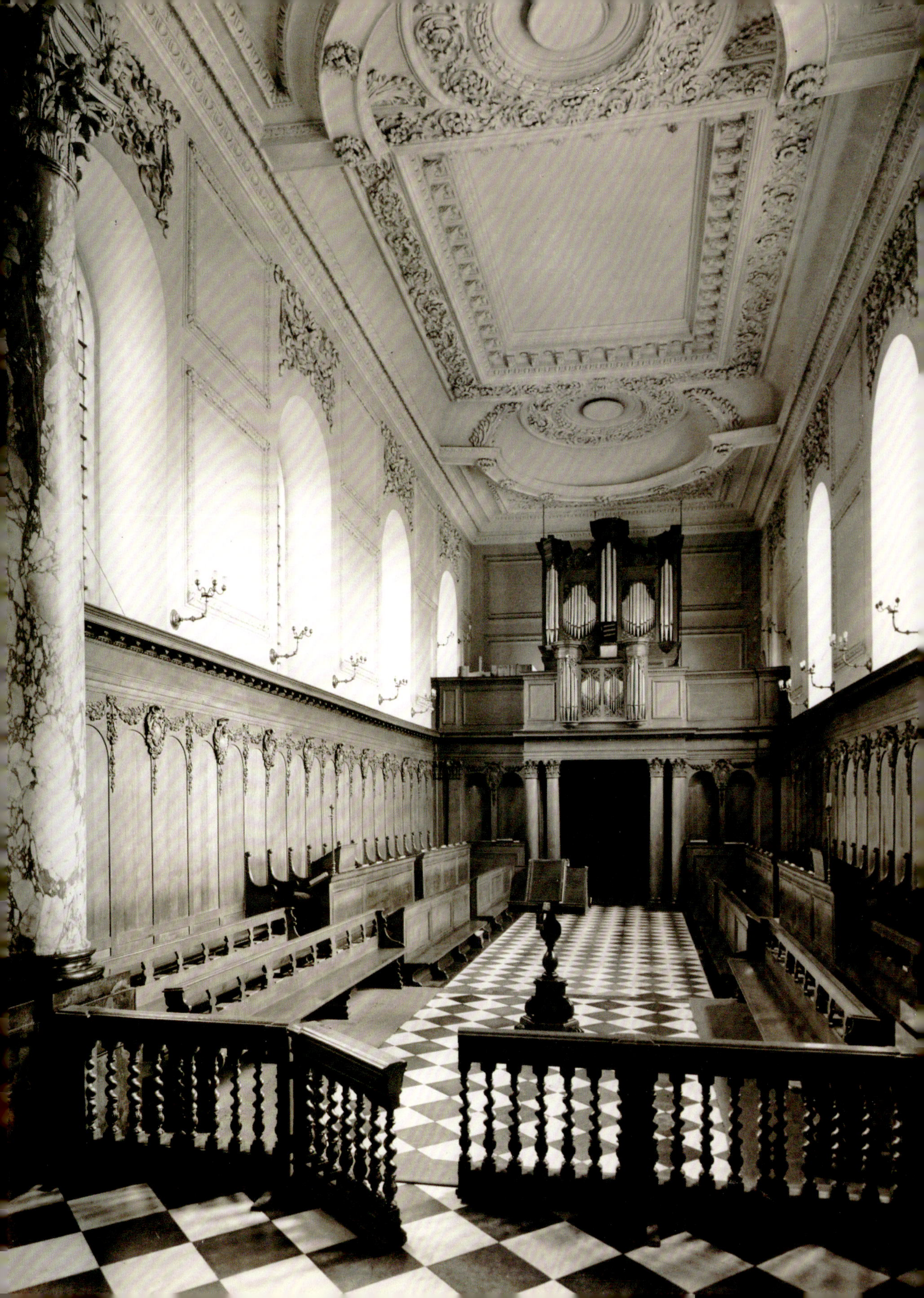

39. Chapel interior, looking west. (*Country Life.*)

40. The framing for the oculus in the organ loft, exposed during repairs in 1979. (Pembroke College Architectural Archive.)

strongly lit main body of the chapel, while striking, is therefore unlikely to have been intended by Wren.[146] Similar apertures occur in St Paul's cathedral.[147] The oculus was probably closed off by 1847, since Storer's engraving of that date, of the interior looking west, does not suggest light flooding into the ante-chapel.[148] The closure of the oculus was probably dictated by the nineteenth-century enlargement of the organ beyond its modest Baroque proportions.

The chapel: overall plan

The chapel itself was originally an undivided space. The western two-thirds of this – the body of the chapel – was fitted out with stalls and benches that remain largely in their original state. The east end – none of which could be used to seat the congregation – accounted for about a third of the area of the chapel (see Scott's plan of the original chapel, Fig. 4). It was raised above the level of the body of the chapel by three shallow, black- marble steps, the lowest of these being separated from the other two by a small area of black-and-white marble paving (Figs 4, 54). The first of these steps was presumably the extra one introduced to minimise seepage of water into the vault (see p. 55). The communion rails were at the top of the third step and extended the full width of the chapel. The altar was at the far end of the chapel, below the east window. The east end was further differentiated from the body of the chapel by a difference in the character of the wood-carving, to be described below.

It seems likely that, while Wren would have been responsible for making this simple overall plan, he would have been subject to strong outside

---

146 The oculus is indicated in a survey drawing of the chapel in *Building News*, 3 May 1907, Fig.70. It is not clear how the surveyor (W H MacLucas) knew of its existence at this time.
147 Gordon Higgott, personal communication.
148 In Charles Henry Cooper, *Memorials of Cambridge* (Cambridge, 1866).

influences in doing so. The planning of a college chapel at this period would have taken place in the context of the prolonged controversies of previous decades about the configuration of parish churches. One of the practices that Archbishop Laud and his colleagues had tried to stamp out was the placing of the communion table lengthwise in the body of the church, with the communicants sitting around it. Instead, it was to be placed at the east end, with its short ends facing north and south, thereby becoming an altar. There were to be rails, either across the full width of the chancel or around three sides of the altar, at which the communicants were to present themselves. Enrichment of the east end of the church or chapel was encouraged, as was the introduction of all manner of liturgical objects. As Kenneth Fincham has suggested, the adoption of this configuration at Pembroke would have followed inevitably from Wren's close connections with the Laudian hierarchy, which included not only his uncle (the bishop) and his father (Dean of Windsor and a distinguished churchman) but the two eminent Laudians responsible for Wren's next commissions after Pembroke chapel: Gilbert Sheldon, Archbishop of Canterbury, donor of the Sheldonian Theatre, and William Sancroft, Master of Emmanuel College, Cambridge, later Dean of St Paul's and Archbishop of Canterbury, and the initiator of Emmanuel chapel.[149] The high-Anglican Laudian ideals had already been realised in Cambridge by 1634 in Peterhouse chapel, the building of which Matthew Wren had initiated (p. 9).[150] After the Restoration and his own reinstatement as Bishop of Ely, he resumed his campaign to introduce these ideals into the churches of his diocese and would certainly have insisted that his new chapel at Pembroke should be laid out along these lines.

Fincham has also drawn attention to the fact that, after the Great Fire, when fifty-one of the parish churches of the City of London were rebuilt, the accounts, approved by the commissioners responsible for the rebuilding, show that 'the arrangements at the east end followed a standardised format: the communion table was to stand on a black and white marble floor, resting on a black marble step, sometimes with a second plain step . . . All were also railed, and most backed by an altarpiece.' The arrangement of the east end of Pembroke chapel is almost precisely that later adopted in the City churches.[151] Wren could not know it at the time, but Pembroke chapel was a trial run for the designs for churches which would subsequently flow from the Wren office.

These ecclesiastical considerations no doubt dictated in a general way the layout of the interior and particularly of the east end, but they had to be

---

149 Kenneth Fincham, 'According to ancient custom: the return of altars in the Restoration church of England', *Transactions of the Royal Historical Society*, 13 (2003), 29–54.
150 For Peterhouse chapel see Graham Parry, *Glory, Laud and honour: the arts of the Anglican counter-reformation* (Woodbridge, 2008), 77–9.
151 And also in Emmanuel College chapel.

translated into the reality of the building. There is no evidence to show how far Wren was involved in this. Craftsmen commonly played an important part in design as well as execution at this period; we have already seen evidence for Edward Pearce's probable role in the design and execution of the decorative stone carving. The interior of the chapel is to a large extent a matter of wood, shaped by joiners and wood-carvers, and it is their work that must now be discussed.

Woodwork and wood-carving: the body of the chapel

Looking back from the east end of the chapel (Fig. 39) almost everything that one sees of the woodwork is essentially as it was in the seventeenth century. Oak panelling of uniform design extends throughout the interior. The panels are tall, rather narrow, round-headed and only slightly recessed within plain framing, entirely without mouldings. Above them there is a deep cornice, almost continuous around the chapel. Before Scott's extension was built, this uniformity of the interior would have been even more pronounced, for his survey drawing (Fig. 53) – published here for the first time and revealing the east end in its original state – shows that the same panelling then continued without interruption from the side walls up to the reredos. Scott retained this panelling, but his new arch broke the continuity. Although the panelling gives every sign of having been executed in one campaign of work, it may not all have been completed by 1665, for as late as 1687 the College chapel accounts show payments for 'wainscotting and carving' (see further below).

The ambience of the different parts of the interior is largely created by the style of the wood-carving, applied to the panelling throughout the chapel. The building is small but the carving is complex, and distinct styles occur in the body of the chapel and at the east end. Evidence will be presented to show that the carving is the work of more than one craftsman and that, while the carving in the stalls was probably completed by 1665, at least some of the work at the east end was not finished until at least the 1670s.

In the body of the chapel the seating is set in three descending rows, interrupted by two gangways on each side (Fig. 4). In the uppermost row there are fourteen seats on each side. These all have scrolled arm rests and desks in front and were intended for the fellows (they are still designated thus). Each is backed by a single panel. Below there are two rows of benches for the undergraduates, the upper of them with desks in front. The module of the panelling, equal to and perhaps determined by the width adopted for the stall-seats, is unrelated to that of the windows above, a slightly jarring feature, once noticed, suggesting that here the design of the interior and the main structure of the building were handled separately. It will be suggested that the stalls were probably not designed by Wren. At the east end, these spatial relationships are more satisfactorily handled, as we shall see.

The upper rows of seats return along the west end of the chapel to provide two further seats on each side. Traditionally, the Master sits here on the south side, the President (Vice-Master) on the north. These seats, somewhat grander than the rest, take the form of semi-circular niches with semi-domed tops (Fig. 39), like those on the west front of the chapel (Fig. 19). They are created within the thickness of the screen separating the chapel from the ante-chapel (Fig. 4), which, as we have seen, also supports the organ loft. The screen, together with the paired Corinthian columns just in front of it, which frame one's first view of the chapel interior and create a suitably impressive entrance into it (Fig. 80), perhaps constitute the most sophisticated piece of design in the building.

Drawings. The contract with the joiners, to be examined shortly, refers to a 'certaine forme and draught of Joyners work' which is (or are) not known to have survived. However, there is important related material that must now be discussed.

For the chapel at Emmanuel College, Edward Pearce was paid £2 'for delineating the Ground plot and Wainscott and Seates in 5 Severall Draughts'.[152] As at Pembroke, these drawings have not survived. However, in the collection of Wren and Wren-associated material at All Souls College, Oxford, there is a sheet containing an elevation and section of chapel stalls, without any indication of what building they are for (Fig. 41).[153] Stylistically, and also from the handwriting in an inscription on the back, the drawing has been identified by Gordon Higgott as being by Pearce.[154]

The drawing shows three descending rows of seats, just as in the stalls of both Pembroke and Emmanuel chapels. Such a configuration, however, would be expected in any collegiate or similar chapel. Some precise dimensions are indicated on the drawing, which, in some respects, appears to be a working drawing. However, some features appear provisional: the desk in front of the middle row of seats, for example, seems to be placed so close to them as to make access difficult.

Comparing the drawing with the stalls in both of the Cambridge chapels, there is an obvious difference in that it shows deep canopies over the upper

---

152 Emmanuel College Archives, Chapel Building accounts; Stubbings, *Emmanuel College chapel*, 10. The payment, which was made by 1676, is specifically to 'Mr Peirce of London'. Some confusion has arisen previously from the presence in the same archives of a copy of a letter about measurements of the chapel dimensions, in which the writer, the Master of Emmanuel, Thomas Holbech, invites the unidentified recipient to name a time when 'Mr Peirce and Mr Oliver may meet and confer with you about the delineations wch have been shown you here'. 'Mr Oliver' is taken to be John Oliver, who was primarily a surveyor but worked also as architect and designer. There is, however, no record of a payment to him at Emmanuel and nothing to suggest that he had any part in designing the stalls.
153 Geraghty, *Architectural drawings*, 23, no.7; AS IV, 90. (Also *Wren Society*, vol. 9, pl. 43.)
154 Gordon Higgott, personal communication.

41. Design by Edward Pearce for chapel stalls, for an unidentified building. Note the canopies above the stalls and the animal feet.
(All Souls College, Oxford; Geraghty, *Architectural drawings*, no. 7.)

tier of seats, present in neither building. Apart from this, the drawing might suggest that the upper seats are to be separated by arm rests, whereas in Emmanuel chapel this seating is in the form of a continuous bench. Again, at Emmanuel, the panelling backing the stalls is made up of rectangular panels with bolection mouldings, of which there is no sign in the drawing. There are arm rests at Pembroke, but there the module of the seats and panelling (27 inches) is larger than that shown in the drawing (24 inches). Such differences make it difficult to sustain Anthony Geraghty's tentative suggestion that the drawing might be a preliminary design for the Pembroke stalls.[155]

The inscription on the back of the drawing also seems to preclude this being a preliminary drawing. In Pearce's hand, it reads, 'Mr Phillips to bring a designe of ye festones ye Arches to the Architraue & to giue ye thickness for ye stuffe to be Cutt outt'. This suggests that the carving was about to be put in hand and that the building for which the stalls were intended must therefore have been well advanced.

The identity of Mr Phillips is uncertain, if only because there is more than one candidate. One is Andrew Phillips, Christopher Wren's clerk and a member of the staff of Wren's office. The earliest record of him in this capacity appears to be in 1675 in the early accounts for St Paul's, where he signs a receipt for Wren's salary.[156] His name subsequently crops up in the building accounts and other records for several of the City churches until 1686, when he was succeeded as Wren's clerk by Hawksmoor.[157] If this identification

---

155 Geraghty, *Architectural drawings*, 23.
156 For Andrew Phillips see *Wren Society*, vol. 10, 93.
157 Geraghty, *Architectural drawings*, 11.

were correct, Pearce's drawing would most probably be for a Wren building, and that cannot be Pembroke chapel, for Wren's office was not in existence by 1663–65, when the chapel was being built. Alternatively, and perhaps more plausibly, Mr Phillips might be Henry Phillips, a leading London joiner, who was appointed 'Master Sculptor and Carver in Wood' at the Office of Works in 1661 and died in 1693, when he was succeeded by Grinling Gibbons.[158] Pearce's statement on the back of the drawing is consistent with the interpretation that Phillips, as the leading carver in the Office of Works, would be the man supplying the design for the carving, as Gibbons did later. This does not, of course, tell us what building the drawing was intended for, but it does make it unlikely that it was for either Pembroke or Emmanuel chapels, for there is nothing to connect either building to the Office of Works, or Henry Phillips to Cambridge. Whoever Phillips was, the most likely possibility is that the drawing was for an unidentified, now-destroyed chapel royal.

However, Pearce's drawing is important for present purposes in confirming what the Emmanuel College accounts tell us, namely that he was competent to provide a design for chapel stalls. It also tells us something about how carving was put in hand in those days. Mr Phillips is seemingly to bring (presumably to the joiners) the design for the carvings on the stalls so that the necessary wood for them can be cut out, to be carved elsewhere by someone else. We shall see shortly that this is how the carving was also handled at Pembroke. Wood-carving seems often to have been done off-site at this time (as it would mostly be today). For example, at Coleshill (designed by Sir Roger Pratt, completed in 1662) 'festoons' carved in London by Richard Cleere were 'sent down in a basket',[159] while at Sudbury Hall, Derbyshire, where Pearce was responsible for much wood-carving, Beard and Knott could find no archival evidence that he ever visited the house.[160]

Finally, and most importantly, there is an intriguing and probably significant resemblance in a point of detail between the drawing and the stalls at both Emmanuel and Pembroke: in all three, some or all of the seats have clawed animal feet. At Pembroke there are sixteen such feet on the stalls (Fig. 42); at Emmanuel there are fourteen (Fig. 43). As well as drawing such feet, Pearce is known to have carved them. In the building accounts for the London church of St Andrew's, Holborn (1684–90), where he worked both as mason contractor and wood-carver, his bill for carving includes the item 'ffor Carving 2 Lyon's ffoot. £0 –10 – 0'.[161]

---

158 See H M Colvin (ed.), *The history of the King's works* (London, 1963-82), vol. 5, Appendix D, 473 and passim. This identification of Henry Phillips was first suggested to me by Geoffrey Beard and is supported by Geraghty, *Architectural drawings*, 23.
159 Gunther, *Sir Roger Pratt*, 157.
160 Beard and Knott, 'Edward Pearce's work at Sudbury'.
161 *Wren Society*, vol. 10, 103.

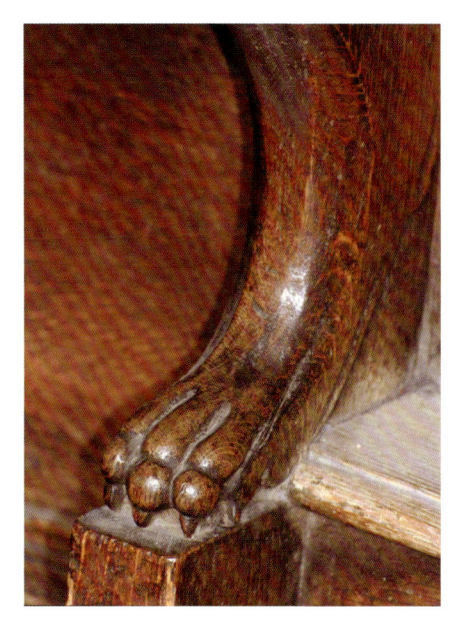

42. Clawed animal foot from Pembroke chapel stalls. (Ian Fleming, 2007)

43. Clawed animal foot from Emmanuel College chapel stalls. (Ian Fleming, 2007)

From all this, it does not seem unreasonable to conclude that Pearce could have provided the design for the Pembroke stalls. The clawed feet give a first indication that he may also have worked as a wood-carver at Pembroke – a possibility that will shortly be examined further. The contract for the Pembroke woodwork, given below, is dated 10 January 1665, so Pearce's 'draught' (if it was he who provided it) must have been have been made by then. Carving would have followed in the same year. The date would fit well with the '1665' appended to the 'E P' in the vault (Fig. 30).

The contract for the woodwork. The record of the agreement made between the joiners and the College for providing the chapel woodwork is the most detailed and informative surviving document about the building of the chapel: it merits quotation in full.[162]

> Articles of Agreement, had made concluded & agreed upon the tenth day of January in the sixteenth yeare of the Reigne of our Soveraigne Lord Charles the Second by the grace of god King of England Scotland France & Ireland, Defendr of the faith &c. Anoq Dom: 1664 [i.e. 1665 in modern reckoning]: Betweene the R[t]. Wor[l] Robert Mapletoft Mast[r] or Keeper of the Colledge or Hall of Mary Valence commonly called Pembroke Hall in the university of Cameb[r] and Nathaniel Coga Fellow of the said Colledge on the one part, and Cornelius Austine and Richard Billopps and William his sonne of Cameb[r] in the county of Camebridge Joyners, on the other part, as Followeth, viz.

162 The contract is in PCA, Hardwick F4. Previously printed in Willis and Clark, vol. 1, 155–56.

Imprimis it is agreed between the said parties . . . First, that they the said Cornelius Austine and Richard and Willm Billopps . . . shall at their owne proper cost and charge find, provide and prepare such a parcell of good cleane and substantiall wainscott, well seasoned all and without any cracks or flaws, as may be every way fit and sufficient for the Joyners work wh is to be done and sett up within the New Chapell at Pemb. Hall in Camebridge, and that whatever parcells of the said wainscot shall be thought to be insufficient and any way defective the said Robt Mapletoft and Nath. Coga shall have liberty to refuse the same, and they obliged forthwth to supply better in the stead thereof.

Item it is agreed that they . . . shall at their own proper cost and charges prepare work and sett up all the said wainscott according to a certaine forme and draught of Joyners work agreed upon between the said parties with 14 seates on each side the chappell, and two returning on each side the doore beneath the organ loft, and with a large Cornice all round that inner Chappell: and the whole work (at least within the inner chappell) to be finished, so as that the said inner chappell shall be in readinesse for the laying of a marble pavement before the dedication of the said chappell, wh is intended to be upon the 21st of September next after the date hereof, yf god permitt. Item that they . . . shall at their oun charges provide all materialls of good wainscot for the two Rowes of the lower seates descending from the upper seates and answering thereunto, and for the carved work within the said chappell viz. for the Festoones and for the Capitalls.

Item it is agreed that the price to be paid by the said Robert Mapletoft and Nath. Coga unto the said Cornelius Austine and Richard and Willm Billopps shall be five pounds twelve shillings and six pence for every of the forenamed seates (being in all thirty two seates) with the two outer seates answering unto them, wh are included in that said price wh is agreed upon for the thirty two seates.

Item that they . . . shall provide . . . all the groundwork, ioyces, stepps, and Floores of all the said seates into the same rate and price of £5 . 12s . 6d per seate excepting only some odd remnants of oak y^t remaine about the work of the said chappell, wh the said Robert Mapletoft and Nath. Coga are to allow them for the groundwork. Item that they the said Joyners shal make such a difference for the seates on each side the doore beneath the organ loft as the said Robert Mapletoft and Nath. Coga shall direct them.

Item that the price to be paid unto them the aforesaid Joyners for the Cornice from the ends of the seats around the East end and also over the doore to the inner chappell shall be sixteen shillings per yard to be measured by the girt: they to find all materialls and work belonging to it. Item the price to be paid for every round Columne shall be three pounds for the materialls of it and working and finishing all belonging to it except the Capitall.

Item it is mutually agreed that they . . . shall deduct and make allowance unto the said Robt Mapletoft and Nath. Coga for the avennues and passages where the seates are to be interrupted at the rate of twelve shillings per yard girt measure. Item that the said Robt Mapletoft and Nath. Coga shall allow unto them the said Joyners twelve shillings per yard for the wainscot in the Corners of the chappell next under the organ loft with the Cornice over it to be measured by the girt. Item it is agreed that the price to be paid for the wainscot in the outer chappell, to be wrought with large faire pannells and Balection molding shall be seven shillings per yard girt measure, and they the said Joyners to find all materialls belonging to it.

Lastly for the times of paym^nt it is covenanted and mutually agreed that in consideration the said Cornelius Austine and Willm and Richard Billopps shall give good and sufficient security for the several summes they shall receive untill their work be performed according to these articles, that then the said Robert Mapletoft and Nath. Coga shall pay unto them the Joyners aforesaid one hundred pounds the tenth day of March next after the date hereof, and fifty pounds more the tenth day of Aprill, and fifty pounds more the last of June next comeing, and the rest as soon as their work is in due manner fully compleate and ended. In witnesse whereof the parties above mentioned have hereunto interchangeably set their hands and seales the day and yeare first above written.

Memorandum. It was agreed before the sealing that the price to be paid for the Pillasters in the door passage and the outer chappell shall be 12^s per yard girt measure.

Sealed and delivered in the presence of
H Brunsell Will. Sampson   Robert Mapletoft Nath Coga

Cornelius Austin was the master joiner for the chapel. The Austins were a Cambridge family, three generations of which were joiners. Cornelius (1622–c.1699) was the senior member of the family and the foremost Cambridge joiner of his day. He worked in nine of the Cambridge colleges, including King's, Emmanuel and Trinity.[163] Skilled joinery, such as that mainly dealt with in the contract, no doubt constituted the bulk of his work, but there is evidence of his ability as a carver in both Emmanuel chapel (see Fig. 52) and, much later, with growing skill, in the Wren Library at Trinity College, where he was responsible (c.1695) for one of the delicate limewood carvings of benefactors' coats of arms on the bookcases, scarcely distinguishable from those of Grinling Gibbons, which Austin followed closely. The other workmen mentioned in the contract, Richard and William Billopps, were members of a family, three or four generations of which appear repeatedly in the Pembroke accounts, receiving payments for a variety of jobs, including carpentry. As we have seen, both Cornelius Austin and one of the Billopps

---

163 I am indebted to Robert Williams for information about the Austin family.

participated in Matthew Wren's funeral procession (p. 1) – appropriate acknowledgement of their work in the chapel and of the long employment of the Billopps family at Pembroke.

Robert Mapletoft signs the agreement for the College as Master, with Nathaniel Coga as a fellow (he was to succeed Mapletoft as Master). Of the witnesses, H Brunsell is almost certainly Henry Brunsell, who was not a fellow of Pembroke but a prebendary of Ely. He was married to Anne Wren, sister of Christopher Wren and therefore niece of Matthew Wren, under whom Brunsell enjoyed a flourishing ecclesiastical career in the diocese of Ely.[164] He was probably representing Matthew Wren's interests as donor. William Sampson was a fellow and Treasurer of Pembroke at the time and the initials 'W S' in the chapel vault are probably his.

Four points in the agreement call for comment:

(a) Although woodwork runs through the entire interior of the chapel, the document concentrates almost wholly on the west end – that is, the body of the chapel. The layout of the stalls and benches, of the steps and gangways between the seating, are dealt with in detail. The 'round Columne(s)' that are mentioned occur only at the entrance into the chapel from the ante-chapel. There is no reference at all to the arrangements at the east end, no mention of the reredos or communion rails.

(b) Referring to the stalls, the agreement refers to a 'certaine forme and draught of Joyners work', implying (not unexpectedly) that there is a drawing or drawings of these. The description of the work to be done is indeed so detailed that it could only have been based on drawings.

(c) While rates of payment for panelling, cornice and seats are set out at length, the agreement makes no mention of rates of payment for carving. It states unequivocally, however, that the contractors are to supply the materials for 'the carved work within the said chappell viz. for the Festoones and for the Capitalls' and, further, that 'the price to be paid for every round Columne shall be three pounds for the materialls of it and working and finishing all belonging to it *except the Capitall*' [italics added]. All this agrees with what is envisaged in the inscription of Pearce's stalls drawing. It seems clear, therefore, that contrary to the assumptions of the Royal Commission on Historical Monuments, Cambridge volume[165] and of Esterly,[166] Austin was not at this stage envisaged as the carver. Why should he supply himself with wood for the carved work if he were then to carve it? Someone else must have been expected to do that. However, we shall see later that, despite this, Austin was almost certainly responsible for some of the less important carved work on the stalls.

164 See C S L Davies, 'Conspiracy, kinship and preferment in the Interregnum and Restoration: the Brunsells and Holders of Nottinghamshire', *Midland History*, 31 (2006), 1–17.
165 RCHM, *Cambridge*, part 2, 154.
166 David Esterly, *Grinling Gibbons and the art of carving* (London, 1998), 74–5.

44. General view of the carving above the stalls. The two types of cartouche are shown, with one of the foliated pendants between them and the linking festoons of flowers and foliage. (National Monuments Record.)

(d) The document is dated 10 January and requires that

> the whole work (at least within the inner chappell) [i.e. the chapel itself rather than the ante-chapel] [is] to be finished so as that the said inner chappell shall be in readinesse for the laying of a marble pavement before the dedication of the said chappell, [which] is intended to be upon the 21st of September next.

Completion of the whole of the chapel woodwork within about nine months, less the time needed to lay the marble floor, seems a tall order. It suggests a degree of urgency on the part of the College – understandable given Matthew Wren's age – for the chapel to be finished quickly, so that it could be consecrated on the next St Matthew's Day (see p. 112) and also prepares us for the fact that the chapel was probably not finished by that time.

As with the contract for the brickwork, the document makes no mention of Christopher Wren.

Wood-carving in the body of the chapel. The carving here is mostly that for which the joiners agree in their contract to provide the wood. On stylistic grounds, a date of about 1665 seems appropriate for this; if it was not all in place when the chapel was consecrated, it is all in the style of that period. This generalisation certainly applies to the carving in the stalls but can probably be extended to the Corinthian capitals of the columns and pilasters at the entrance into the chapel (Fig. 61). These, it may be noted, are of conventional pattern and do not resemble those of the chapel exterior or of the reredos (see below).

The decorative work of the stalls is elaborate and prominent. The overall design (Fig. 44) is that, in the spandrels between the panels, large cartouches alternate with simple, beribboned foliated pendants, all linked by festoons of

45. Cartouche of the 'cherub and foliate head' type. (Christopher Hurst, 2008)

46. The second type of cartouche, in auricular style: a grotesque variant of that in Figure 45, with animal masks at top and bottom, satyr profiles to left and right. (Ian Fleming, 2007)

flowers and foliage. There are also pendants below the cartouches. Because the cartouches are wider than the pendants with which they alternate, the linking festoons cannot be centred over the panels below. All of the carving is cut from separate blocks of wood, nailed to the panelling.

Two levels of expertise can be discerned here. The cartouches are carved with notable freedom and virtuosity, while the festoons and pendants are much less skilfully done. Avray Tipping noted this difference, describing the festoons as 'close-pressed and lumpy'.[167] There is little undercutting here and the leaves and flowers are often not fully freed from the block of wood from which they are carved. Some of the work here seems unfinished. Corresponding to these stylistic differences, the festoons and pendants are all of oak, while the cartouches are of a different wood, identified by Tipping as being probably elm.[168] It seems clear that two carvers were at work here, a point to which we will return. John Evelyn, about this time, wrote of elm wood that, among many other uses, it is good for the 'Carver, by reason of the tenor of the grain, and toughnesse which fits it for all those curious works of Frutages, Foleage, Shields, Statues, and most of the Ornaments appertaining to the Orders of Architecture'.[169]

---

167 H Avray Tipping, *Grinling Gibbons and the woodwork of his age (1648–1720)* (London, 1914), 44.
168 Ibid., 42.
169 John Evelyn, *Sylva, or a discourse of forest trees* (London, 1670), 33.

The cartouches merit special attention. They are of two distinct types, which alternate along the length of the stalls. In the simpler type (Fig. 45) a central boss, reminiscent of a turtle shell, is surmounted by a winged cherub set below a shell hood. At the bottom, in sharp contrast, there is a grotesque frowning mask with gaping mouth, deep-set narrowed eyes and cheeks framed and formed by leaf-like strands: a form – a foliate head or green man – of much antiquity.[170] There are three such cartouches on each side of the stalls and a larger version of this type occurs on the pairs of stalls at the west end, which each have one. The carver's skill is beautifully shown in the variation of the cherub's heads, only about 10 cm high (Fig. 47). No two are alike: each has its own expression, its own hairstyle. This looks more like the work of a sculptor than of a journeyman carver following a pattern.

The other type of cartouche (Fig. 46), alternating with that just described, is at first not readily interpreted. The plain central boss surrounded by a wreath of laurel leaves is obvious enough, but the remainder initially seems no more than a vigorously carved array of sinuous scrolls. However, closer inspection reveals that this type of cartouche is a bizarre variation on the first type. At the bottom, in place of the foliate head, one makes out an altogether more grotesque animal head: the mouth is a gaping square hole, the nose a small sharply projecting beak, the eyes beady and close-set. Similarly, at the top, in place of the cherub, there are the snout, nostrils and eyes of a dog- or pig-like animal mask. Additionally to these, on each side, towards the bottom of the cartouche and facing sideways, there is a severe, frowning, satyr-like profile. That these features are at first difficult to make out is because they are in large part both formed and obscured by the carved scrolls: the concealment of the masks or heads, animal and human, is deliberate.[171]

47. Montage of cherub heads from the 'cherub and foliate head' type of cartouche. Note the differences in proportions and expressions, and the freedom with which the hair is carved. (Ian Fleming, 2007)

170 See, for example, Kathleen Basford, *The green man* (Ipswich, 1978).
171 Almost none of the regular users of the chapel was aware of them.

The wood-carving of the stalls is hybrid in character, with two distinct styles in juxtaposition.[172] The festoons and pendants are standard forms of the first half of the seventeenth century. Entirely classical in style, they might have come from a building by Inigo Jones or his follower John Webb, and they are common on furniture of that period.[173] The cartouches, and especially the second type, represent something different: they are the work of someone familiar with the auricular style, already referred to in relation to the carving in the west pediment (p. 70) but here more obviously apparent.

The auricular style (its name derives from the similarity of its curved, melting forms to those of the human ear) is, in its fully developed form, characterised by refinement, virtuosity, artificiality (with a corresponding departure from naturalism) and the introduction of the grotesque.[174] It had its origins in Italian Mannerist decoration of the sixteenth century. From there it was taken up by northern-European designers, particularly Dutch gold- and silversmiths, from whom it spread, during the seventeenth century (by engravings as well as actual examples), to ceramics, glassware and the carved ornament of furniture and picture frames.[175] The auricular style is 'anti-classical': later it would be one of the sources of rococo decoration. In England it is represented chiefly in memorial tablets and cartouches in churches, in picture frames of the 1660s to 1680s[176] and, in printed work, in the engraved title pages of books and the framing of dedicatory panels on engravings. It is difficult to find parallels elsewhere in England to the extensive use of it as a decorative element in Pembroke chapel.

Who was responsible for the remarkable cartouches? Edward Pearce was a skilled wood-carver. There is persuasive stylistic evidence that he carved the altar rails at Emmanuel College (see p. 115) and he worked extensively as a carver in the some of Wren's City churches and in important buildings elsewhere. It has been suggested already that he may have carved the animal feet of the Pembroke stalls and it is reasonable to ask whether he was also responsible for the more complex carving there. In seeking support for this suggestion, possible sources for the stalls cartouches may be sought.

It has already been noted that the elder Edward Pearce published what has come to be known as the *Book of friezes*: a suite of twelve engravings of designs apparently intended for plasterwork or carved wooden decoration, first produced in 1640 (Figs 48a and b).[177] These engravings are highly relevant to

172 I am greatly indebted to Alastair Laing for guidance in understanding this carving.
173 See Adam Bowett, *English furniture, 1660–1714* (Woodbridge, 2002).
174 See Simon Jervis, *The Penguin dictionary of design and designers* (Harmondsworth, 1984), 39.
175 For a survey see W K Zülch, *Entstehung der Ohrmuschelstils* (Heidelberg, 1932).
176 For example those at Ham House, Richmond, chiefly dating from about 1673. For a discussion of auricular frames see Jacob Simon, *The art of the picture frame* (London, 1996), 52–6 and 196 n. 25.

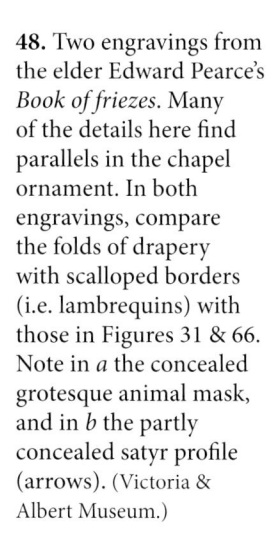

48. Two engravings from the elder Edward Pearce's *Book of friezes*. Many of the details here find parallels in the chapel ornament. In both engravings, compare the folds of drapery with scalloped borders (i.e. lambrequins) with those in Figures 31 & 66. Note in *a* the concealed grotesque animal mask, and in *b* the partly concealed satyr profile (arrows). (Victoria & Albert Museum.)

the wood-carving at Pembroke. They include, in small compass, much of the classical repertoire of the plasterer or wood-carver prior to Grinling Gibbons: festoons of fruit and flowers, urns, putti, acanthus scrolls and the lambrequin (of which those on the wall drawing of the chapel urn (Fig. 31) are almost direct copies). The engravings also draw on the auricular style in their inclusion of some grotesque features. These relate particularly to the second type of stalls cartouche at Pembroke: a grotesque animal head, tucked away and easily overlooked, between two scrolled brackets (Fig. 48a) is strongly reminiscent of the concealed dog-like mask at the top of this type of cartouche. There are also five more-or-less hidden human profiles, one at least partly formed and concealed by scrolls and foliage and closely similar to the satyr profiles of the cartouches (Fig. 48b). The elder Pearce was not, of course, the originator of these motifs. Almost everything he brought together in his engravings could have been derived directly from Continental examples, some of much earlier date. Satyr heads in profile close to those of the cartouches, for example,

177 The title comes from Vertue's description of them as 'a book of Freeze work'. The original plates, with slight alterations, were used for a second printing (also dated 1640). After the elder Pearce's death in 1658 the designs, with minor changes, were twice reprinted from new plates. The first of these new editions is dated 1668, the second is undated but was current before 1672; both still bore the name 'Edward Pearce'. It is not known who was responsible for producing these later editions. Jervis, *'Engraved ornament'*, lists the known locations of copies of Pearce's suite.

49. Engraving by Lukas Kilian (*c*.1630) of an auricular cartouche, with grotesque masks at top and bottom and frowning profiles to left and right, arrows (*cf*. Fig. 46). (Rijksmuseum.)

50. Detail of cartouche from elevation of transept portal, St Paul's cathedral, by Edward Pearce, *c*.1678–85. (Guildhall Library.)

appear in eight of the thirteen engravings by Antonio Fantuzzi (*c*.1540–45) assembled by Berliner.[178] Lion masks, clawed animal feet and urns also occur in them. That the elder Pearce may have known of this source is also suggested by the fact that several of the grotesque motifs in his second set of engravings (see p. 68) can also be found in remarkably similar form in some of Fantuzzi's work. Other examples of engravings, by Cornelius Bos (1506–56), are replete with lion masks.[179] In later work, by Lukas Kilian (dating from 1620–30), we find fully developed auricular cartouches with grotesques at top and bottom and partly concealed frowning profiles to left and right (Fig. 49).[180]

Both of the elder Pearce's sets of engravings were presumably readily available in England and could have been used as pattern books by any carver. The younger Pearce, however, would have had longer and more immediate exposure to them than anyone. He was about five years old when the first set was produced, twelve when the second appeared, and must have known them as a child and youth. He was perhaps responsible for the 1668 edition of the earlier set, produced only three years after the Pembroke carvings.

Given that Pearce probably designed the Pembroke stalls, and given his ability as a carver in wood, it seems reasonable to suggest that he carved the cartouches. They have a sculptural quality and a freedom and virtuosity characteristic of his work: no two of the cartouches are identical. Many parallels can be found in points of detail between the cartouches and Pearce's numerous

178 See Berliner and Egger, *Ornamentale Vorlageblätter*, figs. 289–90, 293–4, 296–7, 300–1.
179 Ibid., figs 640, 642 and 643.
180 Ibid., figs 866 and 867.

church monuments and other carvings. He had a predilection, particularly in his drawings, for placing a face, or mask or grotesque at the top and/or bottom of his cartouches (Fig. 50). Pearce apparently did not again draw on the auricular style to the extent that he seems to have done at Pembroke, but this is characteristic of his work. A famous example of his ability to produce a single work in a style he adopted nowhere else will be discussed later (pp. 117–18).

*

It may be asked at this point whether the cartouches have any symbolic meaning? The question is repeatedly asked by people seeing them and will no doubt occur to some readers. Caution is essential here. On the one hand it could be argued that the stall carvings are no more than a display of the carver's virtuosity, or of his acquaintance with a fashionable style, and that they have no symbolic content. Alternatively, they may have a symbolic meaning, which would have been obvious at the time but to which we have lost the key. The carvings would have been contemplated every day by both fellows and undergraduates, during their obligatory attendance at chapel. Given that Matthew Wren was paying for the chapel, it does not seem too fanciful to suggest that he would have expected the cartouches to embody some meaning and not simply demonstrate a carver's skill.

At a simple level, the winged cherubs may be an allusion to the Biblical description of the temple at Jerusalem, where Solomon 'graved cherubim on the walls'.[181] But what further symbolic content the cartouches might have can only be guessed at. The current practice of art historians is to shun symbolic interpretations of works of art unless there is additional evidence, documentary or otherwise, to support them. No such evidence is available at Pembroke.

If, despite these constraints, one rashly ventures to speculate, the first type of cartouche might yield to a simple interpretation: the grimacing foliate head below could symbolise the sinfulness of the earthly world in which we have our being (signified also by the dark panelling), while the cherub above directs our thoughts towards heaven, symbolised by the ceiling floating overhead, richly decorated with foliage and flowers.[182] And for the second type, in which the imagery is grotesque and unrelievedly severe, one could suggest that after the recent national catastrophes (as Matthew Wren would have seen them) the intention might be to signify that, while for some there was the possibility of salvation (the first type of cartouche), the reality for most was wickedness and damnation.

A passage from an essay by Douglas Bush, referring to the classical-Christian world-view (to which Bishop Wren may be assumed to have adhered) may be apposite here:

---

181 2 Chronicles, 3: 7; a suggestion due to Jayne Ringrose.
182 I owe this interpretation to Robert Ferguson.

This... world-picture had been built up over many centuries, out of traditional philosophy, religion, and the senses and imagination; and, at least in its prime essentials, it was shared by learned and unlearned alike, by Hooker and by Shakespeare. Man could be bestial more often than angelic, but he was God's creature in a world rich in meaning. He knew, if he did not always remember, that he was daily enacting under the divine eye the supreme drama of salvation or damnation. Everyday life was a variegated web of the brutal and the miraculous ... human experience and language and image and symbol comprehended the widest and deepest range of significance and contrast.[183]

At nearly eighty years of age and with a life-time of traditional scholarship and Christian practice behind him, Matthew Wren would have been inclined to look backwards, rather than towards the unfolding scientific world of his nephew. *Paradise lost*, it may be remembered, was published in the year of Matthew Wren's death.

*

By contrast with the cartouches, the festoons and pendants of the stalls are unimaginative and seem most unlikely to be Pearce's work. It has already been noted that they are carved from different wood. During conservation in 2008, many pieces of the stalls carving were taken down for repair. Almost without exception the festoons and pendants examined had the initial 'A' cut on the back (Fig. 51),[184] whereas no initials were found on the cartouches. A plausible explanation of the 'A' would be that, although the contract for the woodwork initially excluded Cornelius Austin from carrying out the carved work, he may have been brought in later to complete the carving in the stalls. The Emmanuel College chapel accounts prove that this would have been well within his powers, for there he was paid for carving Corinthian capitals and festoons (Fig. 52) and later, as noted, he was to produce excellent carving for Trinity College Library.

Confirmation of Austin's role as a carver is perhaps to be found in the College's Chapel Accounts. Although these are totally silent about the chapel's initial construction, they contain many entries about work carried out after its notional completion. In 1687 there is an entry, 'Pd. Mr Austin for Wainscot in the Chappel £40', and in the same year William Billops was paid £15, also for wainscot. In the following year, a sum of £30. 13s. 6d. (recipient not stated) was 'Paid out of the chest beside the £55 accounted for last audit for wainscot, carving etc.' It is not evident what these large sums were for. It is possible, though perhaps unlikely, that they relate to work being done at

51. Initial 'A' inscribed on the back of stalls wood-carving, believed to denote Cornelius Austin. (Robert Williams, 2008)

---

183 Douglas Bush, 'Science and literature', in H H Rhys (ed.), *Seventeenth century science and the arts* (Princeton, 1961).
184 Robert Williams, conservator, observed that the 'A' was in all cases formed by using a V-shaped carving chisel to cut the sloping strokes and a plain chisel to cut the cross-stroke.

that time on the Old Chapel, which was undergoing conversion into a library (see Appendix 2). Assuming, however, that they relate to the New Chapel (as it was for some years called), they tell us that at least some of what Austin received at this time was for carving. Indeed, the wainscotting (that is, panelling) element referred to could not have accounted for more than a small proportion of this expenditure, for at 7s. per yard (the rate in the contract for the woodwork) £85 would have paid for over 240 square yards of panelling, which is more than twice the area of panelling in the whole chapel. A contemporary account of the chapel's consecration described it as 'beautified with a splendid and decorous Furniture' (p. 112, n.), which makes it difficult to believe that the building was largely without panelling or stalls at the time, especially as the contract for the woodwork focuses almost exclusively on these. Completing the less demanding part of the carving in the stalls could well be one of the things that Austin was paid for in 1687–8, though that would require us to believe that the chapel was left unfinished for at least twenty-two years after its consecration. It will be suggested later that he may also have done other carving in the chapel.

A minor, final point to note about the stalls is that, in the upper tier, the seats opposite the four gangways are hinged, with misericords on the underside – more a medieval feature than a Classical one, mitigated by the fact that all four are decorated with identical, stiff acanthus-leaf carving.

Woodwork and wood-carving: the east end

52. Festoon of fruit, with ribbons and drapery swags, Emmanuel College chapel, carved by Cornelius Austin. (Ian Fleming, 2007)

The plain pattern used for the panelling of the body of the chapel continues throughout the east end. Figure 54 shows that, on the side walls of the chapel, the transition between the body of the chapel and the east end was handled, in somewhat perfunctory fashion, simply by a change in the style of the carved decoration, without any other structural demarcation.

The original appearance of the east wall is shown in Scott's survey drawing (Fig. 53).[185] Here, the carefully regulated design is largely based on a relationship between the widths of the windows and the width of a bay of the panelling, the latter being one-tenth of the total width of the wall. This module, 31 inches, is larger than that of the panelling of the stalls, on average 27 inches. The reredos, four panels wide, is flanked by three bays of panelling on each side. The central window of the Serliana above is the same width as the reredos and the side windows are equal to two panels.

185 E H Minns, 'The Wrens' chapel', *PAG*, 20 (1946), 9–14 includes a hypothetical reconstruction of the east end by Denys Spittle, but this assumes (incorrectly) that the reredos was unaltered by Scott.

THE SEVENTEENTH-CENTURY CHAPEL

53. Scott's survey drawing of the east end elevation, before his alterations (see text for description).
(RIBA Library Drawings and Archives Collections, SCGGJ[13]88.)

The cornice at the top of the panelling finishes just below the window sills, with the pediment of the reredos intruding only slightly into the window space – a feature in which the design resembles that of Inigo Jones's Queen's Chapel of St James's Palace (Fig. 23). The Corinthian pilasters on each side of the reredos originally extended down to floor level. At the top, then as now (Fig. 57), the entablature breaks forward above them.[186]

As Figure 54 shows, the communion rails were originally at the junction of the body of the chapel with the east end, and were therefore much further from the east wall than they are now. Nevertheless, the same module was adopted for them, the spacing between the uprights being approximately twice the panel width.

The satisfying unity of the whole composition, almost certainly due to Wren, was disturbed when Scott created the new sanctuary (see p. 125).

Wood-carving of the east end. This is perhaps the least well understood feature of the chapel. There is probably work of more than one period and by more than one craftsman, but insufficient evidence to allow certainty as to

---

186 The painting that now occupies the centre of the reredos – a copy of Barocci's *Entombment*, of which the original is in the church of Santa Croce, in Senigallia, Italy – was not acquired until 1797 and it is not known what was there previously.

THE INTERIOR

54. The junction between the body of the chapel (right) and the east end, before Scott's alterations. The end of the stalls is seen and the upswept end of the communion rails. The carving on the panelling shows the abrupt transition between the last of the cartouches over the stalls, with its heavy festoon of fruit and flowers, and the delicate staff-like pendants and festoons of flowers of the east end. The lectern here is Victorian. (Pembroke College Architectural Archive; before 1880.)

dates and names. The best that can be done at present is to describe what is there and suggest some possible solutions to the problems of attribution.

As noted, the cartouches and heavy festoons of the stalls give way at the east end to a different style of carved decoration. This consists of a much simpler repetitive pattern of thin, staff-like pendants between the panels, linked by delicate festoons, all consisting of flowers and leaves (Figs 54, 55, 56). The basic element of the design, used in both pendants and festoons, consists of a large central flower surrounded by leaves and smaller flowers, often crocus-like. Esterly points out that the larger flowers were carved separately from the rest and attached later.[187] This pattern is carried throughout the east end, along the side walls and onto the east wall, up to the reredos. Compared with the stalls, the carving here is more delicate, less exuberant than that of the stalls: the flowers are fewer, better carved, more widely spaced. They are arranged in slightly varied groupings, but the overall effect is of a repeating pattern. The possible identity of the carver will be discussed later.

The reredos (Fig. 57), the major feature of the woodwork of the east end, is likely to have been built by the joiners at the same time as the rest of the panelling – that is, in 1665. The pilasters on each side are an integral part of the reredos and would presumably have been part of this original work. It seems

---

187 Esterly, *Grinling Gibbons*, 74–6.

THE SEVENTEENTH-CENTURY CHAPEL

55. Detail of one of the pendants from the east end panelling. (James Austin, *c*.1993)

56. Carving of the east end panelling, general view. (Ian Fleming, 2008)

unlikely that their Corinthian capitals would have been left unfinished. These capitals are unusual in style and closely resemble those carved in stone on the chapel exterior (compare Figs 58 and 59); there is the same emphasis on the caulicole and volutes and the same generally wiry character. Those on the exterior, it will be remembered, were attributed to Pearce (p. 70). A drawing by him, dated 1678–79, for a Corinthian capital for St Paul's cathedral (Fig. 60), resembles the two Pembroke examples and would support their attribution to Pearce. If there is a reservation here, it is that the drawing is executed in what Higgott describes as a 'loose, almost painterly' style (similar to that used by him for the cartouche of Fig. 50[188]). The drawing would probably have been made for a mason to follow and we cannot be sure from it how Pearce himself would have carved a Corinthian capital. That apart, the simplest hypothesis, given the striking similarity of the reredos capitals to those on the outside of the building, and of both to Pearce's drawing, is that he was responsible for both. This attribution, however, can at present only be tentative, and its provisional nature is emphasised by the fact that Geoffrey Fisher, taking the carving of the east end as a whole, suggests, on stylistic grounds, a date later than 1665.[189]

The distinctive character of the Corinthian reredos capitals is brought out by comparing them with the very different ones on the columns framing the entrance from the ante-chapel (Fig. 61). In these there is much less emphasis on the caulicole and volutes and they have an altogether less wiry character: they can scarcely be Pearce's work. Given their important position and their

188 Higgott, 'Revised design for St Paul's', dates the cartouche drawing to *c*.1678–85.
189 Personal communication, 2008.

57. The reredos, as altered by Scott. The reredos was raised by an amount equal to the height of the altar and pedestals were inserted below the pilasters, the bases of which were originally at floor level. The bare panelling at the bottom thus exposed was addressed by lowering the picture and inserting a new band of carving above it and three small carved panels below. The drops on either side of the painting are original, as are the capitals and the carving in the pediment. (National Monuments Record.)

58. Pilaster capital of the reredos. (Detail from Fig. 57.)

59. Pilaster capital, west front. (Detail from Fig. 19.)

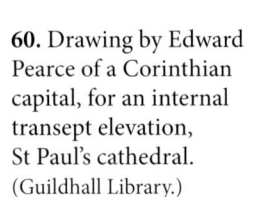

60. Drawing by Edward Pearce of a Corinthian capital, for an internal transept elevation, St Paul's cathedral. (Guildhall Library.)

61. Corinthian capital at the entrance to the chapel from the ante-chapel. (Ian Fleming, 2008)

inclusion in the contract for the chapel woodwork, the columns would probably have been completed by the time the chapel was consecrated (that is, in 1665). Cornelius Austin was responsible for the columns and may have also carved their capitals, notwithstanding that the contract for the woodwork limited him to providing the wood for them.

On either side of the altarpiece on the reredos there are carved drops, with large bows at the top (Fig. 57). As with the carving of the panelling of the east end, flowers are the main component of the drops but here the design is much freer: the flowers are not arranged in tight, evenly spaced groups, but are irregularly distributed and they are attached to a substrate of parallel thin stalks (Fig. 62).

The third carved element of the reredos is the large cartouche in the broken pediment, with fragile, free-floating looped festoons on either side (Fig. 63). The case for Pearce having worked on the reredos carving could seem to be strengthened here, for the cartouche immediately recalls those in the stalls. Here again, the scrolls surrounding the central boss are at the bottom made to frame and partly form a grotesque, flattened human face or mask, open-mouthed and with round staring eyes, while at the top there are the nose and eyes of another severe, frowning, foliate mask. The grotesques and the drooping form of the scrolls are auricular features, as is the placing of the masks at

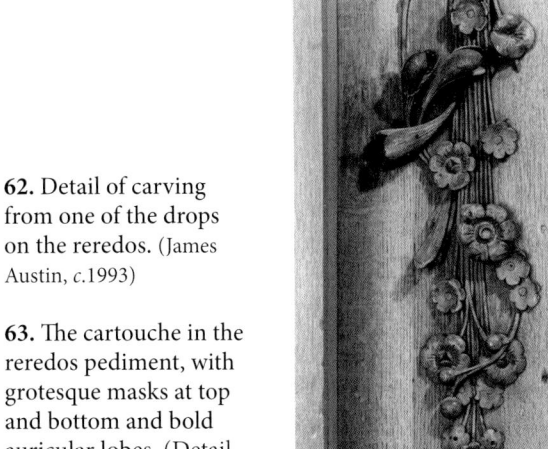

62. Detail of carving from one of the drops on the reredos. (James Austin, *c*.1993)

63. The cartouche in the reredos pediment, with grotesque masks at top and bottom and bold auricular lobes. (Detail from Fig. 57.)

top and bottom of the cartouche, as in auricular picture frames of the period. If the case made earlier for Pearce having carved the stalls cartouches is accepted, the simplest hypothesis, again, is that he was also responsible for the reredos cartouche. If not, we have to invoke the activity of another carver, so far unidentified, with a penchant for grotesque ornament.

All these carved features of the reredos are shown in Scott's survey drawing of the chapel, made prior to his alterations (Fig. 53), suggesting that they belong to the seventeenth-century chapel but not, of course, allowing any more precise dating.

A third example of the grotesque in Pembroke chapel may be introduced at this point. This is the prayer desk, part of the furniture of the east end and the most extraordinary object in the chapel. It carries carved decoration to its limit, for, apart from its sloping top, it is made up of little else, compressing a variety of styles and motifs into a small compass (Fig. 64). Apart from a band of foliate carving on the top rail of the desk, all of the sides consist largely of openwork acanthus-leaf scrolls. This carving is strongly reminiscent of Pearce's work on the altar rails in Emmanuel College chapel (Fig. 75) and of his staircase balustrades at Sudbury.[190] In all of these, too, leaves sometimes sprout from the centre of flowers, as we find in the elder Pearce's *Book of friezes* (Fig. 76). On the legs of the desk the most obvious features are the pendants of carved flowers, attached to parallel arrays of thin stalks. These are very similar to those on the reredos drops, suggesting that the same carver may have been at work. In a complex design, the lower edges of all the sides are each formed by two long curved forms that originate higher

190 Beard and Knott, 'Edward Pearce's work at Sudbury'.

up, among the acanthus scrolls. Although initially plant-like, as they extend down towards the bottom of the legs they swell and become transversely scalloped. At the bottom of each leg we find ourselves looking at the large-eyed, gaping-mouthed head of a dolphin, and realise that the scalloped form just described is its body. As with the grotesque masks of the chapel cartouches, the dolphins are to a degree concealed by the fact that they are partly formed by and integrated into the flowing forms of the openwork foliage. Each dolphin actually has two bodies, since the same design occurs on the sides, as well as the front and back, of the desk: eight bodies to four heads. And by now it can scarcely surprise us that, since a leg needs a foot, each dolphin spouts from its mouth a large animal foot, reminiscent of those of the stalls, though without the clawed toes.

As with the carving on the stalls, classical and auricular motifs are brought together on the prayer desk in a hybrid design. The acanthus-leaf scrolls and the flowers on the legs belong with the festoons and floral pendants of the stalls and the east end, but the dolphins spouting feet recall Pearce's predilection, elsewhere in the chapel, for the grotesque. The line of argument linking the reredos cartouche to Pearce would apply equally to the prayer desk.

The carving on the reredos and the prayer desk seems to be linked by common features. There are possible reasons, admittedly not decisive, for suspecting Pearce's hand in its making. If he participated to this extent in the carving of the east end, might he also have been involved in the carving applied to the general panelling of the east end? His role there might have been that of designer, rather than carver, for there is much repetitive work here. Given the large payments to Cornelius Austin for 'wainscotting and carving', noted above, perhaps he was the carver.

The communion rails are the final major feature of the east end. Figure 53 shows that these originally extended across the full width of the chapel. Following Scott's alterations, the central sections alone now survive in situ (Fig. 65). The elegant upturned ends (one is just visible in Fig. 54), for which there was no room in Scott's scheme, are now in the church of St Mary, Tarrant Hinton, Dorset, a Pembroke College living. The rails are formed mainly of helical balusters, set into top and bottom rails which are moulded and decorated with foliated carving. There are broad uprights at intervals, decorated on the front with carved flowers attached to bundles of thin stalks, as on the reredos and prayer desk, but perhaps less freely carved: the stalks are more rigidly in parallel, the flowers less varied. The balusters are in the form of both right- and left-handed helices, used in alternating groups of four or six, with half-helices (balusters sliced down the middle) against the uprights (Fig. 65).[191] Each baluster ends at the bottom in a decorated base with foliate carving.

---

191 The half-helices are present in the ends of the original rails at Tarrant Hinton and are not a result of Scott's alterations.

THE INTERIOR

The balusters provide evidence for dating the rails. 'Twist-turned' components such as these were introduced into English furniture-making in the early 1670s, when lathes (based on the screw-cutting lathe of the metal worker) obviated the need for laborious hand-carving. From then on much fashionable furniture (chair frames and table legs in particular) would be at least partly

64. Prayer desk (see text for description). (National Monuments Record.)

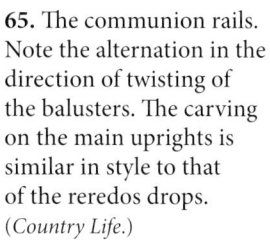

65. The communion rails. Note the alternation in the direction of twisting of the balusters. The carving on the main uprights is similar in style to that of the reredos drops. (*Country Life*.)

turned.[192] Bowett finds that, while some of these components would have been made by independent turners, the larger joiner's shops would have had their own lathes. The Pembroke balusters would certainly have been lathe-turned and therefore cannot have been made before the early 1670s. This dating agrees with the fact that, by the 1670s, twist-turned balusters occur frequently in various contexts in the London City churches. Altar rails very similar to those in Pembroke chapel are (or were) to be found in two of Wren's churches: St Stephen, Coleman Street and St Stephen, Walbrook.[193] The balusters themselves are nearly identical in all three but in the City churches the rails are as a whole more elaborate and more highly finished than those at Pembroke. On the uprights the carved flowers are set within frames and the bundles of thin stalks found at Pembroke are not present. Overall, however, the similarities in design of the three sets are more striking than the differences. In the two churches, the carving on the communion rails (along with much of the other carving) was the work of William Newman. Those in St Stephen, Coleman Street date from 1676,[194] those in St Stephen, Walbrook from 1679.[195]

There is another similarity between woodwork at St Stephen, Walbrook and Pembroke, in that they have very similar lecterns. In both there is a stem of unusual design, with two bold swellings (Fig. 39), mounted on a hexagonal base with acanthus decoration and animal feet. Of the two, the Pembroke version is inferior: it looks like an unfinished or not very competent copy of the St Stephen's version. The Pembroke communion rails, therefore, might be similarly based on those at St Stephen's. In that case a date for them in the late 1670s would seem possible. Given the Laudian insistence that the altar should be set behind rails, it would be surprising if they were lacking at Pembroke when the chapel was consecrated in 1665. The most likely explanation is that the altar rails of the old chapel were used as a temporary measure.

Who made the Pembroke rails is unknown. We have noted that Pearce's altar rails for Emmanuel College chapel (*c*.1678; Fig. 75) were based on open-work acanthus scrolls; this was also the case with his very similar rails at Winchester College (*c*.1680). However, in 1676 Pearce had worked at Wolseley Hall, Staffordshire (now demolished), where he certainly executed the woodwork of the dining room and is believed to have also been responsible for the staircase.[196] The balustrades of this massive staircase were filled with twist-turned balusters, and the design was very similar to that of the Pembroke and London communion rails. The scale of this staircase makes it obvious that it

---

192 Bowett, *English furniture*, 72–4.
193 The former church was demolished after suffering bomb damage in 1940, but photographs of the altar rails are reproduced in *Wren Society*, vol. 10, Photographic Supplement, 32.
194 Geoffrey Beard, *Craftsmen and interior decoration in England, 1660–1820* (Edinburgh, 1981), 273.
195 *Wren Society*, vol. 10, 120 n. 196.
196 Robert Plot, *Natural History of Stafford-shire* (Oxford, 1686), 383.

would have been quicker and cheaper to fill the balustrades with ready-made balusters than with many yards of hand carving, a consideration that would probably also have been relevant at Pembroke. These are more joiner's than carver's jobs. Pearce's role in devising the staircase would probably have been mainly as designer and as overseer of the joiners who put it together. Just possibly he was similarly employed at Pembroke.

We are left with an inconclusive story about the carving at the east end of the chapel. Several clues seem to connect it to Pearce, but there is no decisive evidence. He died in 1695 and went on working nearly to the end of his life. The possible lateness of the east end carving, might be explained if Pearce returned to work in Pembroke chapel long after 1665.

Plasterwork

There is decorative plasterwork on both the walls and the ceiling of the chapel.

Wall decoration. On the side walls, the spaces between the windows are articulated by pairs of rectangular plaster panels, one above the other, outlined by bolection-moulded frames enriched with foliage. Together they extend from panelling to ceiling (Fig. 39).

More interestingly, the spaces above the windows, including the west window, are filled with identical elaborate compositions (Fig. 66). The principal feature in each is a mask (or mascaron), open-mouthed and (seen from below) with upturned eyes, surmounted by a foliate headdress and with transversely ribbed bib-like drapery below. The bottom edge of the drapery is pleated and irregularly scalloped, as are its folded sides: it is, in other words, a lambrequin. From ceiling height, the masks appear much longer and narrower than when seen from floor level: they have been skilfully modelled to allow for the foreshortening (Fig. 67). All are slightly different, resembling in this respect the cherub heads of the stalls.

66. Plasterwork wall decoration above a window, photographed from floor level. Similar decorations are present above all of the side windows and the west window. The ribbons and lambrequins resemble those in the wall drawing of the urn (Fig. 31). (Pembroke College Architectural Archive.)

THE SEVENTEENTH-CENTURY CHAPEL

67. Detail of the mask from a wall decoration, photographed from ceiling level. The proportions and features have been sculpted to create the appearance from floor level shown in Figure 66. The side edges of the bib-like drapery are serrated (i.e. it is a lambrequin). (Ian Fleming, 2007)

68. A mask with a lambrequin bib, from the elder Edward Pearce's *Book of friezes*. (Victoria & Albert Museum.)

A festoon of leaves, flowers and fruit extends on each side of the mask with, at each end, a hanging pleated fold of drapery with a decorative border – another lambrequin, this time in the typical form previously encountered in the wall drawing for the urns on the chapel roof (Fig. 31). The curling ribbons in the urn wall drawing are also present in the wall decorations, identical in treatment but here extended so as to fill the remaining space of the composition. In these features the similarities between the urn drawing and the wall panels are so marked that the attribution of the latter to the same designer – and hence, in all probability, to Pearce – seems plausible.

Some other considerations would support the attribution to Pearce. First, the wall decorations display the same hybrid nature as the wood-carving of the chapel stalls: classical festoons frame a less obviously classical mask. Secondly, while such masks, sometimes with a lambrequin below, occur occasionally in Continental engravings of grotesque ornament, the example that would have been closest to hand for Pearce would have been the one that occurs in his father's *Book of friezes* (Fig. 68).

As we shall see, there are no obvious stylistic similarities between the wall decorations and the ceiling: they appear to be the work of different designers and probably different plasterers. If Pearce designed the wall decorations, it is possible that he also made them. He was a sculptor and would have modelled in clay in making bronze busts (for example, that of Oliver Cromwell[197]). Pearce worked as mason and carver at the City church of St Clement Danes and it has been suggested that 'he may have been a modeller in plaster if the profuse ornamentation of [that church] is due to his large share in that work'.[198]

Ceiling. The elaborate ceiling, which survives in its original state, is comparable in quality to the wood-carving. It is complex in structure and its effect derives from bold shaping in depth, coupled with finely modelled mouldings and foliage: it is both restrained and rich (Fig. 69).

The ceiling runs uninterrupted over the full (original) length of the chapel. Its large central area, extending over most of the width and much of the length of the building, is raised about five feet above the two shaped end panels (Fig. 70). Its rounded ends are slightly greater in circumference than a semicircle, the acute inner edges accentuating the effect of depth (Fig. 71). Within this main central area there is a large recessed rectangular panel enclosed within an elaborate cornice and an outer framing of richly scrolled foliage.

At the ends of this, at the same level, are circular panels, around which the framing of foliage continues. The shaped end panels of the ceiling contain long branches of bay,[199] framed within a border of bay leaves, and there are other foliated branches extending upwards at the four corners of the coved central area. The latter feature is also present in the Emmanuel chapel ceiling, which, as a whole, in its coving, richly detailed cornice, bay-leaf framing and foliated scrolls, is strongly reminiscent of the Pembroke ceiling. It differs in being divided by cross-beams into three unequal bays, corresponding to the organ gallery, nave and sanctuary, thus remedying the possible defect in design of the Pembroke ceiling, which continues without break over the organ loft.

It is unlikely that a ceiling of this confidence and complexity would have been devised solely by Wren. As with the rest of the building, he would have depended on published designs and on his craftsmen. French sources seem likely. One of Jean Le Pautre's designs for ceilings, for example, shows a large central rectangular panel set in a surround with semicircular ends, just as at Pembroke. Also among the same set of designs there are sections of small buildings (tombs, etc.) with deeply coved ceilings, which may have suggested the coving of the Pembroke ceiling.[200]

The stylistic resemblances between the ceilings of Pembroke and Emmanuel chapels suggest that the same plasterer was responsible for both. It is known that at Emmanuel this was John Grove, who submitted his bill, dated

---

197 In the London Museum.
198 *Wren Society*, vol. 10, 93.
199 So identified in RCHM, *Cambridge*, part 2, 153.
200 See nos 1834, 2165 and 2166 in M Préaud, *Inventaire du fonds français: graveurs du XVIIe siècle* (vol. 12): Jean Lepautre (part 2), (Paris, Bibliothèque Nationale, 1999).

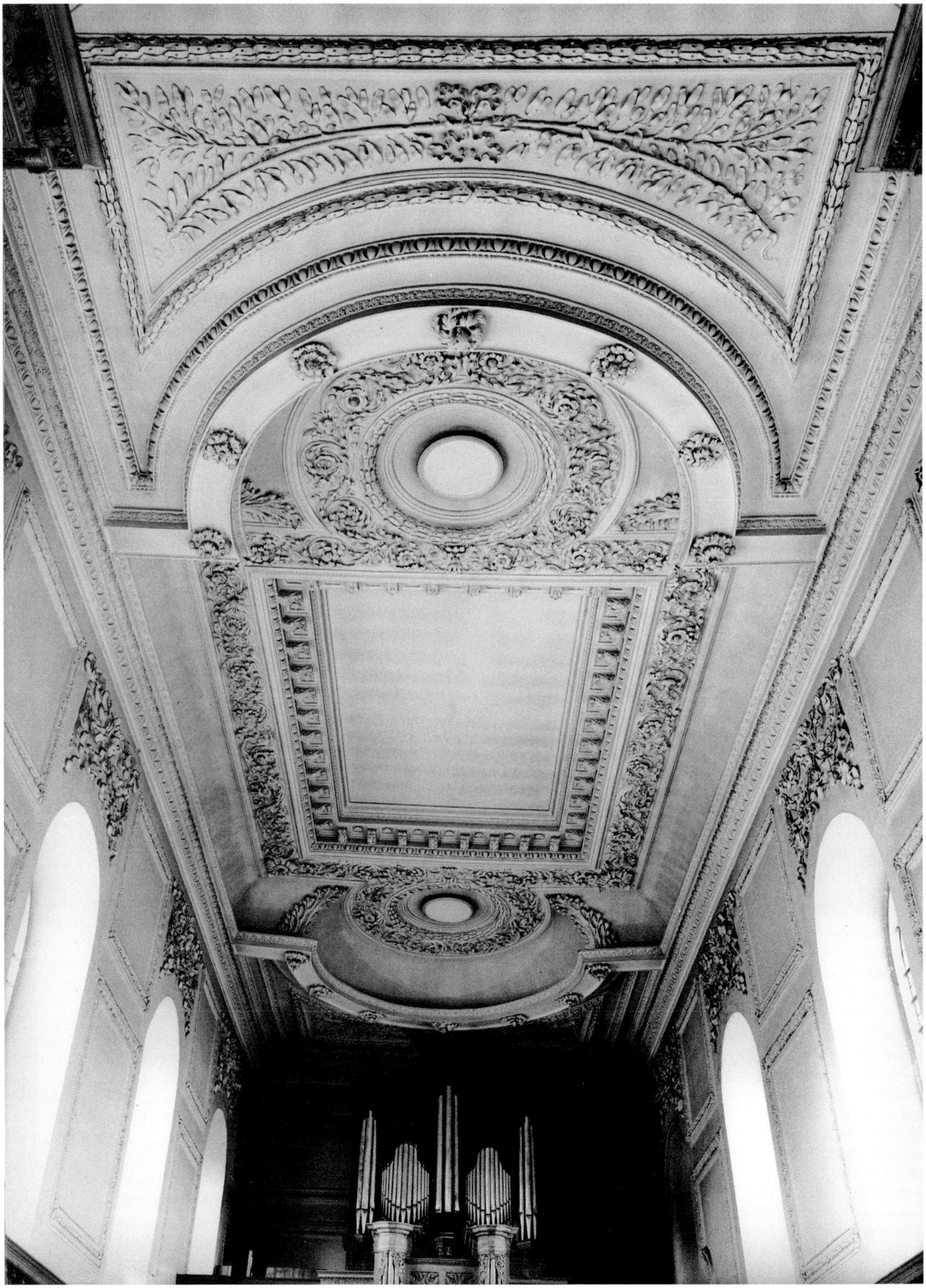

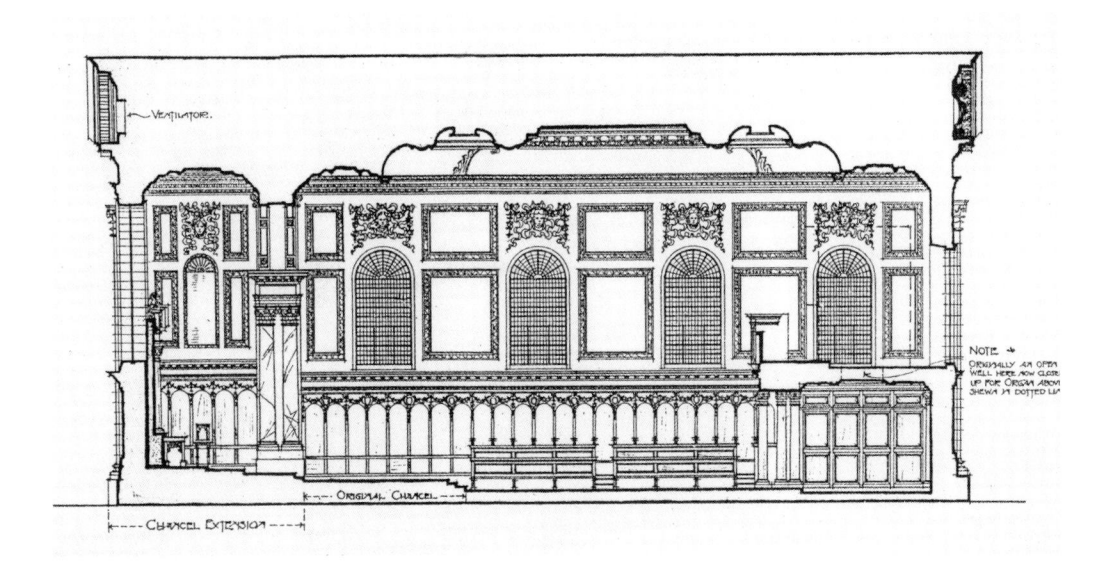

69. (left) Chapel ceiling, general view, looking west. Wall decorations above the windows are visible to left and right. (National Monuments Record.)

70. Section of the chapel (after the building of Scott's extension), by W H MacLucas. Apart from showing the deep coving of the ceiling, the drawing provides an excellent depiction of the overall form of the interior, (From *Building News*, 3 May 1907.)

4 July 1672, of £260 for plastering the chapel walls and ceiling.[201] Fortunately, Emmanuel evidently questioned the amount claimed and initially paid Grove only £140. The matter was evidently not quickly settled for over two years later, in December 1674, we find him (again in the Emmanuel College Archives) submitting a justification of his original claim based on a comparison of the areas of the walls and ceilings of the Pembroke and Emmanuel chapels, together with evidence ('by Mr Coga's Letter', Coga being then a fellow of Pembroke) that he had been paid £192. 13s. 0d. for his work at Pembroke, on which basis he should have received £241. 9s. 6d. from Emmanuel.[202] The outcome of the dispute is not recorded.

While this proves that the same plasterer was responsible for both chapels, it does not immediately settle who that was, for there were two John Groves, father and son, both plasterers, whose careers overlapped and who are known to have sometimes worked together.[203] The elder Grove was, however, much the more notable craftsman. His name appears repeatedly as the plasterer of Wren's City churches, often working in collaboration with Henry Doogood. Before that he worked at the Queen's House, Greenwich (1661) and for Sir Roger Pratt at Clarendon House, Piccadilly (1664–7): important commissions from around the time of Pembroke chapel. He died in 1676. Beard attributes to him (possibly assisted by his son) all plastering work prior to that date for which 'John Grove' received payment.[204] His son's career is obscure and it is not known when he was born or when he began work. He would

---

201 Emmanuel College Archives, Chapel 1.1.4 (2).
202 Emmanuel College Archives, Chapel 1.1.4 (4).
203 For example, at St Mary-le-Bow church in the City; *Wren Society*, vol. 10, 51, 62 and 64.
204 Beard, *Craftsmen and interior decoration*, 262–3.

71. Detail of east end of the ceiling. (Ian Fleming, 2008)

probably have been a young man in 1664, when the Pembroke ceiling was executed, and it is almost inconceivable that Wren would have entrusted him with two such major jobs (Pembroke and Emmanuel) while his father was still alive. There can be little doubt that John Grove senior was the plasterer in question.

It is interesting to find that Grove's justification for payment by Emmanuel College is based simply on the areas of plasterwork, at '10s. a Yarde' (that is, a square yard) for ceilings and 3 shillings for walls. There is no reference to the complexity of the mouldings and other features of the ceilings. He also makes no mention of the wall decorations at Pembroke: nine quite large and complex features which could surely not have been charged for at the rate of 3s a square yard. Either Grove was paid separately for these or, as has been suggested above, someone else was responsible for them.

The bill for plastering at Emmanuel includes £30 for carpenter's work, no doubt required for the complex timber framework of the ceiling. Some idea of the labour-intensive nature of constructing a large lath-and-plaster ceiling is given by the charges for 90 bundles of laths at 2s. a bundle and 50,000 nails.

Paving

The chapel is paved with black and white marble squares, laid diagonally (as at Emmanuel chapel), with black marble edging (Figs 39, 54, 79). The steps (from the ante-chapel and at the east end before the communion rail) are

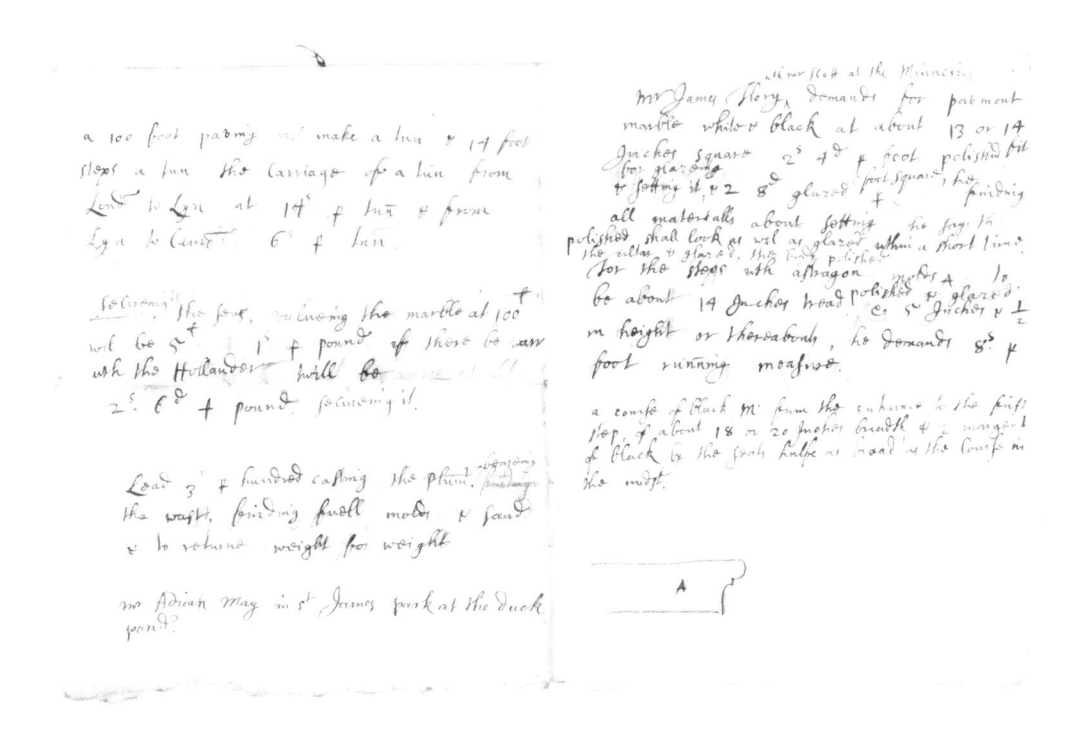

72. Wren's notes on the marble flooring of the chapel. (PCA.)

also of black marble. The paving is important not so much in itself but because some notes about it were, until recently, the only piece of documentary evidence for Wren's involvement with the building of the chapel. They also provide further evidence that he relied on the same team of craftsmen for both Pembroke and Emmanuel chapels. The document was published by Peter Meadows, on whose paper the following description is based.[205]

The document (Fig. 72) came to light in the College Archives in 1994 and contains notes about the quantities, costs and procurement of the marble and about the design of the floor. These were written on the back of a sheet containing the draft of a codicil to Matthew Wren's will, apparently being used as scrap paper. The notes were probably written at Ely House, London (Matthew Wren's London residence) in late 1664 or early 1665 and gathered up with other documents (including the preliminary drawing) and brought to Pembroke after the bishop's death. The notes were written in pencil and later carefully inked over. It is 'extremely probable' that the handwriting is Wren's.[206] The notes read:

> A 100 foot paving will make a tun & 14 steps a tun. The Carriage of a tun from Lond[on] to Lyn at 14s per tun & from Lyn to Camb[ridge] 6s per tun.

---

205 Meadows, 'Sir Christopher Wren'; PCA, Hardwick E6.
206 Identification by Kerry Downes, in Meadows, 'Sir Christopher Wren'. Gordon Higgott (personal communication, 2009) confirms this identification and suggests that the inking over of the writing may have been done by Wren.

Secureing it the Seas, vallueing the marble at 100£ will be 5£. 1s per pound if there be warr w[i]th the Hollander twill be…at…2s 6d per pound, secureing it.

Lead 3s per hundred, casting, the plum[be]r beareing the waste, finding fuell, molds & sand & to returne weight for weight.

Mr Adrian May in St James park at the duck pond.

Mr James Flory w[i]th Mr Scott at the Minneries demands for pavment marble, white & black at about 13 or 14 Inches square 2s4d per foot polished fit for glazeing & setting it, & 2s 8d glazed per foot square, he finding all materials about setting. He says the polished shall look as wel as glazed w[i]thin a short time, the altar &c glazed, the body polished. For the steps w[i]th astragon molds A to be about 14 Inches tread, polished & glazed, & 5 Inches & ½ in height or thereabouts, he demands 8s per foot running measure.

A course of black in from the entrance to the first step, of about 18 or 20 Inches breadth, & 2 margent[s] of black, by the seats halfe as broad as the Course in the midst.

These read like notes jotted down by Wren as an aide-memoir of a meeting with an artisan, probably James Flory, a London mason who would later supply the marble floor for Emmanuel College chapel.[207] The reference to Adrian May – brother of the architect Hugh May and inspector of Royal Gardens in London – is probably an unrelated reminder noted down by Wren and has nothing to do with the marble. 'Securing it the Seas' means insurance in transit, which would cost more if war with the Dutch broke out again, as it did in the summer of 1665.

Insignificant though it may seem, this is an important document in the chapel's building history, for it shows Wren to have been closely involved with both details of design and procurement of materials. Wren's concern with matters that might be expected to be in the hands of, say, the mason contractor, suggests that his role was not confined to architectural matters. There may also be an indication here that there was some anxiety about the cost of the building.

The contract for the chapel woodwork (p. 80) stipulated that it should be finished in time for the floor to be completed before the proposed consecration of the chapel on 21 September 1665. The floor would therefore have been laid in the late spring or summer of that year.

The ante-chapel is paved with squares of limestone (probably Portland stone), laid diagonally and with small, black slate or marble squares inset at alternate corners (Fig. 4).

---

207 Stubbings, *Emmanuel College chapel*, 10.

THE CLOISTER AND THE VESTRY

When the chapel was substantially complete work began on linking it up to the rest of the College by a new range running along Trumpington Street, with a cloister below and two floors of rooms above. This was finished by Christmas 1666. The cost (£466. 19s. 4d.) was met with money from Sir Robert Hitcham's benefaction.[208] His arms are displayed in a panel on the court side at first-floor level. The cloister originally took up the full width of the building at ground level (Figs 4, 73) and was bounded towards Trumpington Street by a wall that followed the medieval pattern of Old Court, a door giving access to the street (Fig. 2). Towards the court side there was an arcade of four bays with squat square piers and Tuscan pilasters (Fig. 5). The door to the chapel was adjacent to the west (street) side of the cloister (Fig. 73). Access to the rooms above was gained via staircases at each end of the range, contained in square, flat-roofed structures (fore-buildings, as the Royal Commission on Historical Monuments volume calls them), partly within the cloister, partly projecting into the court, as Scott's survey drawings show (Figs 4, 73). Scott demolished them. It is not known whether Wren was involved in the design of this range: it called for and displays no notable architectural skill. A very similar arcade is shown in Anthoine Le Pautre's *Les Oeuvres d'architecture*, of which Wren owned a copy.[209]

The completion of the chapel and the cloister left an untidy area between the chapel, the south range of Old Court and the Master's Lodge. The 'Old Hostle' that occupied part of this site was now pulled down and the southern (interior) face of Old Court was tidied up. The effect was to create a small third court (additional to Old Court and Ivy Court), which became known as Chapel Court. As Loggan's engraving (Fig. 2) shows, there were certainly some buildings within this court, adjacent to the chapel. The available evidence does not show conclusively what these were but the Chapel Accounts provide clues; what follows is an attempt to deduce what the arrangements might have been.

---

208 Willis and Clark, vol. 1, 147.
209 Antoine Le Pautre, *LesOoeuvres d'architecture d'Anthoine Le Pautre* (Paris, 1652; reprinted Farnborough, 1966), Discours Cinquieme, 'Veiie de l'enclos du partaire de L'Hotel to Monseigneur le Marquis de Fontenoy Mareuille'. Wren's copy is recorded in Watkin, *Sale catalogues*, lot 563.

73. Scott's survey drawing, showing the western end of the chapel before his alterations, with the cloister range in section. The entrance into the chapel is shown in its original position, close to the street side of the cloister. Abutting the window, is one of the two flat-roofed structures containing the stairs giving access to the rooms above the cloister. (RIBA Library Drawings and Archives Collections, SCGGJ[13]89.)

It is known that, in 1669, a staircase was made leading down from the upper part of the Master's Lodge into this court.[210] Loggan offers two possibilities for this staircase: it could either be the open staircase shown descending into the court from the little loggia at first-floor level, or it could have been contained within the narrow building, with pitched roof and buttresses, abutting the Lodge: perhaps the former is the more likely. Between the narrow building and the chapel, Loggan shows a small flat-roofed building. The entrance to the vault lies below where that building is shown. It is presumably to this flat-roofed building that the Chapel Accounts refer in recording a payment, dating from some time prior to September 1668, of 'An arrear to

210 Attwater, *PAG*, 7 (1933), 17–19.

the Bricklayer for taking down the chymnies adjoining to the Vault and making up the wall, £4. 5s.', for 'chymnies' seem to imply a building and 'adjoining to the Vault' necessarily means close to the chapel. Entrance into the vault at present is via a small stone slab let into the ground adjacent to the chapel and necessitates an awkward manoeuvre under the bottom of the chapel wall. It would not have allowed either coffins, or the large slabs of stone making up the sarcophagi, to be taken down. The original opening must have been much larger, and one may guess that there was originally a stairway, enclosed within the flat-roofed building, allowing a coffin to be carried down into the vault with reasonable propriety. Payments in 1717 to a bricklayer, plumber, carpenter and glazier for 'repairing the Vault' suggest that this covered entrance was originally regarded as part of the vault, for it is difficult to explain why the services of at least the latter three tradesmen could have been required in the vault itself, which contains neither lead, wood nor glass.

There are also references at several points in the accounts to the vestry. For example, in 1677 there are payments 'For mending the Vestry: Smith 100 of nailes, 2s. 6d.; The carpenter £4 3s. 8d; The plummer £6 16s. 6d.; Stone-cutter 1s.'. It seems probable from this that the flat-roofed building, perhaps built initially to enclose the vault entrance and regarded as part of the vault, may also have served as a vestry. Ideally, this would have communicated directly with the chapel, and there is some evidence for this, for an appropriately placed relieving arch in the brickwork below the west jamb of the last window (Fig. 74) suggests the existence of a doorway here,[211] and a payment in 1707 'To Richard Lee for walling up the Door Place between the Chapel and Vault' also seems to confirm the existence of this entrance.

74. Relieving arch in the north wall of the chapel, believed to indicate the position of a former door giving access to the chapel from the vestry. (James Austin, *c.*1993)

A doorway in this position, giving access to the original east end of the chapel, would, of course, have necessitated an opening in the panelling, of which there is at present no sign. As we have seen (p. 90) there were payments for wainscotting in the chapel as late as 1687, and some of this expenditure may have been for taking out the internal door and door-frame and replacing them with plain panelling. The date, however, does not fit particularly well with the date of 1707 for the walling up of the doorway noted above, requiring the internal door to be removed twenty years before the doorway through the brickwork was filled in.

211 RCHM, *Cambridge*, part 2, 153 supports this explanation.

CONSECRATION

As planned, the chapel must have been sufficiently near completion by 21 September 1665 (St Matthew's Day) for Matthew Wren, once again Bishop of Ely and now aged eighty, to come to Pembroke on that day to perform the service of consecration. His nephew was not present, for Wren had left towards the end of June for the long visit to Paris that was to give him his only first-hand acquaintance with the architecture of the Continent.

Seated before the altar, attended by the Master, Robert Mapletoft, and by his second son, Dr Thomas Wren, Archdeacon of Ely, he read out the Act of Consecration.[212] In Latin, it begins with an expression of praise to Almighty God for having been delivered from the squalors of imprisonment in the Tower, and for the fact that he can now see before his aged eyes ('prae oculis senilibus') the chapel that he vowed to give, and that he can now offer to God. It is consecrated under the name of the New Chapel ('Novum Sacellum'). In a separate ceremony, 'before Evening Service', the ante-chapel and cloister were consecrated as places for the interment of fellows or students, 'together with a Cell [i.e. the vault] at the East end of the Chappel under the Altar, for a Dormitory for his Lordship'.[213]

Matthew Wren was to die less than two years later, on 24 April 1667. His funeral has been described in the Prologue. In his will he left to the College silver from his own chapel at Ely House, Holborn (candlesticks, a chalice, patens, flagon and alms dish), together with a set of twenty-nine stall cushions.[214] The cushions may, like the silver, have come from his chapel, though since their number agrees very nearly with the number of the chapel stalls, and their design suggests that they were made in the seventeenth century, they may have been made to Matthew Wren's order for the new chapel. They bear the arms of Ely impaling those of Wren.

212 PCA, Hardwick E3.
213 Willis and Clark, vol. 1, 621, quoting from *The Intelligencer*. The same source relates that 'The Vice-Chancellor, and several Masters of Colleges, the Heads of the University, with the Dean and Canons of *Ely*, were present at this sacred Solemnity; which was celebrated with signal Instances of a high devotion'. This account also refers to the chapel's 'splendid and decorous Furniture', and notes that 'by the blessing of a singular Providence all the Colleges have hitherto continued without any suspicion of Contagion' – there had been outbreaks of plague in Cambridge during the building of the chapel.
214 The cushion covers are of knotted pile fabric (i.e. made in the same way as an oriental carpet) and were probably made in Norwich, a known centre for such work in the sixteenth and seventeenth centuries.

CONCLUSION

The strongest immediate influence on the outward form of Pembroke chapel is that of Inigo Jones. His example would have prompted the use of a Roman design (deriving from Serlio) for the west front, and his own buildings were the basis for the Serliana of the east end and the design of the side elevations (again deriving from Jones's studies of Palladio and Serlio). Wren was ultimately responsible for bringing together these diverse sources to create the overall shape and design of the exterior, but apparently he did not begin the design process, for the preliminary drawing of the north elevation, in which Jonesian influences are clear, is by Edward Pearce. He, it has been argued, probably also designed the stalls, had a major input as the designer and carver of stone and wood, and may also have contributed to the decorative plasterwork.

Comparison with Emmanuel College chapel

For Emmanuel chapel (1667–73), which followed closely on Pembroke's, Wren had a less difficult site, with much greater architectural potential, for the new chapel was to be the centre-piece of a new east range of the college's main court. In his design, according to Pevsner, 'Wren worked with Italian motifs exclusively, but using them in an oddly unclassical way. Pembroke chapel is much purer in the new classical style than the later Emmanuel chapel'.[215] Probably this was the effect of his visit to Paris in 1665. His plan, in which the chapel is flanked by colonnades to left and right, with rooms over, is at first sight close to that at Peterhouse, built for Matthew Wren about forty years earlier (see p. 9), but at Emmanuel what we at first take to be the west front of the chapel is, in fact (again in Pevsner's judgement), 'a sham', for on the ground floor it conceals an open cloister, continuous with the colonnades to left and right, and on the upper floor it fronts part of the Master's gallery: the entrance to the chapel lies behind the apparent west front, within the cloister, and the chapel itself has no external west wall. The lantern, too, does not strictly belong to the chapel, for it is supported on a pedestal bearing a clock, rising through the pediment of the (sham) west front.[216]

215 Pevsner, *Cambridgeshire* (Harmondsworth, 1970), 72.
216 The pedestal rises from a projecting central part of the frieze, causing 'the sides of the pediment to seem to disappear – a decidedly Baroque feature. On the block with the clock rests a big, rather heavy lantern, less elegant than that over the street end of Pembroke Chapel'. (Pevsner, *Cambridgeshire*, 72).

Such vagaries, however, are absent from the interior of the chapel, which is strictly, almost austerely, Classical. As at Pembroke, the plan is a simple rectangle, with the ante-chapel below the organ loft. As already noted (p. 71), the Pembroke ceiling plan, unbroken from east to west, has been adjusted at Emmanuel to give separate compartments over ante-chapel and sanctuary. The large, round-headed windows of the sides are the same in both chapels, but in Emmanuel there is no east window. The stalls are similar in design, but the wood-carving, largely confined at Emmanuel to small Corinthian capitals and modest festoons, lacks the exuberance of Pembroke's. There are no plasterwork wall decorations. Instead of a communion rail stretching the full width of the chapel and dividing it into two, the altar is surrounded on three sides by altar rails and placed against the east wall in a much smaller sanctuary. The effect is to make the body of the chapel a larger and more coherent space. The floor in both chapels is of black-and-white marble throughout.

In the short period between the design of the two chapels Wren was on a steep architectural learning curve. In Emmanuel chapel, one can see him both absorbing the lessons of designing his first two buildings (Pembroke chapel and the Sheldonian Theatre) and also reacting to his exposure to Continental architecture. Emmanuel chapel is, as a result, a more complex building than Pembroke's but also a more sophisticated one, particularly in the more unified handling of the interior.

Good records survive of the craftsmen who worked at Emmanuel.[217] The list of craftsmen is closely similar to that provisionally established here for Pembroke chapel. Indeed, it suggests that Wren depended on an almost identical team for the two chapels. None of the craftsmen on these lists, it may be noted, worked on the Sheldonian Theatre, which was being built at the same time and for which Wren assembled a quite distinct team.[218]

The designation of Pearce as 'contributing designer' covers different work on the two chapels. As far as we know, at Pembroke, working prior to Wren, he made a preliminary drawing of the north elevation; at Emmanuel he delineated the ground plot. He designed the stalls at Emmanuel and probably did so at Pembroke.

The wood-carving at Emmanuel was certainly in part the work of Cornelius Austin for, whereas at Pembroke he was only to supply wood to be carved by someone else (p. 82), at Emmanuel his contract provides 'for tenne Large Corinthian Heads Nyne pounds, and for every two small Corinthian heads and a festoon one pound'. The second item here refers to the fact that, in the Emmanuel chapel, narrow Corinthian pilasters are interpolated between each bay of the panelling, with festoons between them (Fig. 52). That Austin

---

217 Stubbings, *Emmanuel College chapel*, 10.
218 The master joiner, for example, was William Cleer, the chief wood-carver was Richard Cleer (both from London) and the stone carver was William Byrd, a local man. See Howard Colvin, *The Sheldonian Theatre and the Divinity School*, 2nd edn (Oxford, 1974).

	Pembroke chapel	**Emmanuel chapel**
Principal architect	Christopher Wren	Christopher Wren
Contributing designer	Edward Pearce	Edward Pearce
Mason	Robert Grumbold (?)	Robert Grumbold
Brick-layers	George Jackson & Thomas Hutton	*Not known*
Stone carver(s)	Edward Pearce (& Robert Grumbold?)	Robert Grumbold (?)
Designer (stalls)	Edward Pearce (?)	Edward Pearce
Carpenter	Cornelius Austin	Cornelius Austin
Wood-carver(s)	Edward Pearce (& Cornelius Austin?)	Cornelius Austin & Edward Pearce
Plasterer(s)	John Grove (& Edward Pearce?)	John Grove
Paving	John Flory	John Flory
Time of construction	May 1663–Sept 1665	March 1668–Sept 1677
Total expenditure	£3658	£3972

was to carve these confirms his ability as a wood-carver and supports the suggestion made earlier (p. 90) that he may have done carving at Pembroke.

However, just as at Pembroke, there is no reference in the Emmanuel accounts to the more complex carving at the east end of the chapel. This was not put in place until 1687, when it replaced earlier temporary fittings. The altar rail at Emmanuel (Fig. 75) is a virtuosic piece of carving, with openwork panels of acanthus leaf scrolls, closely similar to the communion rail at Winchester College chapel and the staircase balustrade at Sudbury Hall, both known to be by Pearce. As already indicated, the acanthus scrolls themselves could have come directly from the elder Pearce's *Book of friezes* (Fig. 76). Pearce's role as one of the wood-carvers at Emmanuel seems certain.[219] His employment there for this special work would support the suggestion that he may have had a similar role at Pembroke.

A general conclusion that emerges from this comparison of the two chapels is that the continuity in both the design and in the craftsmen who brought them into being provides convincing support for both being the work of Wren.

---

219 Peter Inskip, 'Emmanuel College chapel: reordering via restoration', *Emmanuel College Magazine*, 87 (2004–5), 55–81, supports this view.

75. Altar rail at Emmanuel College chapel, attributed to Edward Pearce. (Ian Fleming, 2008)

76. Design for acanthus scroll carving, similar to that in Figure 75, from the elder Edward Pearce's *Book of friezes*. (Victoria & Albert Museum.)

Edward Pearce

If the suggestion made here that Pearce worked at Pembroke is correct, this would be his first collaboration with Wren, a finding of some importance. When it began he probably had at least ten years' experience behind him, for he had almost certainly carried out important work as a wood-carver at Thorpe Hall, built in 1653–54. Other jobs, both as craftsman and designer, must have followed, for by 1661 he was sufficiently established to be commissioned to make designs for the triumphal arches for the coronation of Charles II, and in about 1663 was contributing designs for Kingston Lacy. Both of these commissions came at about the time of his preliminary drawing for the chapel, probably made in 1662. Someone, perhaps Matthew Wren, but more probably Peter Mills, must have had considerable confidence in his abilities for him to be considered as a possible architect for Pembroke chapel. Christopher Wren displaced him but was seemingly very ready to entrust him with important areas of the design and to employ him as a craftsman.

CONCLUSION

Documentary proof that Pearce executed all that is proposed here is lacking but the stylistic and other evidence does seem in sum to be reasonably convincing. That the preliminary drawing for the chapel is by Pearce is not in doubt, and the initials in the vault (unless, improbably, they belong to another 'E P') with their late date – 1665, when the chapel was nearing completion – suggest strongly that he was responsible for something else.

Much still remains to be discovered about Pearce but from what is known it seems fair to say that his work was not notably original. His repertoire of design motifs tends to be limited and most can be traced back to his father's engravings. Urns, for example, recur, often with gadrooned covers, flames, and decoration – typically in the form of swags of drapery – around the bowl. A carving or drawing of a Pearce urn is not difficult to recognise. Likewise, Pearce's treatment of drapery is characteristic, in that he almost invariably draws or carves it with an emphasised border: obviously scalloped if the cloth is spread out, or with a thickened margin if it is hanging in folds, features characterising the lambrequin. These occur repeatedly in Pearce's designs for funeral monuments, for example those to Lady Warburton in St John's church, Chester, and to John Withers and his wife in Arkesden church, Essex, and they are present, superbly cut, in Pearce's virtuosic wood-carving in the Saloon (Parlour) at Sudbury Hall.[220] Lambrequins also feature in the Pembroke wall drawing of the urn (Fig. 31) and in the plasterwork wall decorations, for at least the design of which Pearce may have been responsible. That none of these is a major component of any of these designs perhaps gives them added significance as markers of Pearce's work. Taken individually, these stylistic characteristics would perhaps carry rather little weight as evidence of Pearce's hand. It is their concurrence that is so often persuasive, and it is this that we find at Pembroke.

When, in his sculpture, Pearce produces something that seems different he was probably drawing on a new source. Of the captivating bust he made of Wren in 1673, possibly to mark the latter's knighthood (Fig. 77), Margaret Whinney writes, justifiably, that,

> As a portrait of the greatest man Pierce knew it is extremely sensitive, for it is in no way an official portrait but an intimate, almost tender, presentation of an intellectual who is also a man of broad humanity . . . [It is] probably the best piece of sculpture made by an Englishman in the century.[221]

Yet the composition is more decidedly Baroque than any other of Pearce's portrait busts and Whinney suggests a source for it in Bernini's bust of Louis

---

220 Beard and Knott, 'Edward Pearce's work at Sudbury'.
221 Margaret Whinney and Oliver Millar, *English art 1625–1714* (Oxford, 1957), 255. Elsewhere Whinney judges it 'the most memorable of all the portraits of Wren' (Margaret Whinney, *Sculpture in Britain, 1530–1830* (Harmondsworth, 1964) 46–7).

XIV, which Wren might have seen at an early stage when he visited Paris in 1665. Nicholas Penny, less appreciative, writes of Pearce's bust:

> The drama of such a broad triangular composition . . . and of voluminous drapery, hastily pulled across the chest, with loose shirt, and disordered locks each played off against the other, represent responses to Bernini's portrait bust of Francesco I d'Este (completed in 1651) and its numerous imitators, responses similar to those of the French sculptor Antoine Coysevox. . . . Coysevox's faces are frequently given the alert conviviality we see here.
>
> When the bust is examined in relation to Coysevox's bust of Charles Le Brun . . . it is surely only habit, supported by patriotism, that restrains scholars from wondering whether the Ashmolean's marble is not in fact a copy by Pierce of a lost bust . . . by Coysevox. The marble certainly looks like a copy: the boldness of the conception is simply not matched by an equivalent verve in execution. And it is surely extraordinary that Pierce, had he invented a bust of this sophistication and vitality, should never have achieved anything comparable in his other bust portraits . . .[222]

This does less than justice to Pearce's skill in making a carving that conveys so admirably the 'alert conviviality' of his subject, but is probably correct in suggesting that the originality and sophistication of the conception were not his. He possessed matchless ability as a carver in wood and stone but was dependent on styles that he found elsewhere and was adept at taking up.

*

If the account presented here is accepted, we can see Pembroke chapel as largely the outcome of a collaboration between two greatly gifted men: Wren, a brilliant mathematician and scientist, a giant intellectually but a beginner in architecture; and Pearce, of much the same age but already a master craftsman, familiar with buildings and architecture, with sculpture and decoration, member of an artistic family and conscious of his ability. Perhaps it was too much to hope that this first result of their interaction would be wholly satisfactory. The interior of Emmanuel College chapel, Wren's next building, has a calmer, more restrained atmosphere than Pembroke chapel. There is nothing comparable with the auricular cartouches of the stalls or the plasterwork wall decorations, which at Pembroke combine to give the walls a lively, possibly over-decorated effect, with little unadorned space for the eye to rest on. Perhaps Wren was not wholly satisfied with how Pembroke chapel had turned out and, as a result, became less subservient to the ideas of his craftsmen.

---

222 Nicholas Penny, *Catalogue of European sculpture in the Ashmolean Museum, 1540 to the present day*, vol. 3 (Oxford, 1992), 144–5.

77. Bust of
Christopher Wren, by
Edward Pearce, 1673.
(Ashmolean Museum,
Oxford.)

At this point we may return to the awkward fact with which we began: that Pembroke chapel was omitted from the list of Wren's buildings in *Parentalia*. Perhaps we can now see why this was. If Pearce had done all that is suggested here in bringing the chapel into being, that may have been too much, in Wren's view, to justify him claiming the building as his own. And this seemingly modest disavowal might have been made all the more readily if he was not wholly satisfied with the result.

POSTSCRIPT: GEORGE GILBERT SCOTT'S EXTENSION

Rapid growth in undergraduate numbers in the late nineteenth century (for example, from 43 in 1870 to 122 in 1880), at a time of compulsory daily attendance at chapel, made enlargement of the Wren building inevitable. Alfred Waterhouse, the college's architect from 1870 and designer of four buildings at Pembroke, would have preferred to demolish the chapel completely and replace it with a grander structure. This, he wrote in 1870, might have a campanile 30 feet square to the west

> sufficiently high to be the most conspicuous tower in Cambridge . . . If, on the other hand, the college would prefer to adhere to the present chapel, notwithstanding its defective condition . . . and peculiar position . . . I would suggest that an addition in the form of an Apse be made at its eastward. I am aware, however, that the chapel having been built by Sir Christopher Wren (even though it may lack the excellence one is accustomed to see in the work of that Master) its removal would be a matter of regret to many.

By 1874, Waterhouse was willing to allow the chapel to survive, with a new organ recess on the north side and much beautification of the interior by means of rich decoration of the ceiling and the introduction of Morris/Burne-Jones stained glass.

This was not to come about. Disquiet among the fellows at the hostile public reaction to Waterhouse's destruction of the medieval hall led them to dismiss him as architect and engage in his place George Gilbert Scott junior, a less overbearing figure. Scott was about forty years old at the time (Fig. 78).[223] His output was never to be on the scale of his father's and much of his work lay in the restoration and alteration of existing buildings, which in Cambridge had included jobs at Peterhouse, King's and St John's Colleges and at St Michael's church – work that would no doubt have been known to the Pembroke fellows. The churches that were built to Scott's designs (there were

---

223 Three generations of the Scott family were architects. George Gilbert Scott junior, who worked at Pembroke, was the second of these, son of the much more prolific architect of identical name (builder of numerous Gothic revival churches and chapels, energetic restorer of churches and cathedrals, and designer of the Albert Memorial and St Pancras Station and Hotel). George Gilbert Scott junior was father of Giles Gilbert Scott, architect of Liverpool Cathedral, Battersea Power Station, Cambridge University Library and much else and designer of the red telephone box.

seven in all) were all Gothic in style but he was not averse to Renaissance architecture and was prepared to use it for church buildings. Before being invited to work at Pembroke he had submitted schemes in Classical style for several small ecclesiastical projects elsewhere, most of which had not come to fruition. The extension to Pembroke chapel was to be his only large completed design in Classical style for a church building.

Scott no doubt realised that there was unused space in the area beyond the communion rails – space that could be made over into the body of the chapel if the altar were contained in a smaller area. This might have been achieved simply by moving the communion rails eastwards. He chose instead to create an entirely new sanctuary within an additional bay – a major project, which has been described and discussed by Stamp.[224] The extensive correspondence between Scott and the college about his work on the chapel brings out the interplay on practical matters between architect and client.[225] However, his letters are not particularly revealing of the background of his thinking about the chapel and what he planned to do, Scott perhaps judging the fellows as unlikely to be receptive to such considerations.

The new bay (Fig. 5) increased the overall length of the chapel by approximately 17 feet. Its north and south sides are clad in ashlared Ketton stone and the east side is simply the original east wall, together with its clasping pilasters, taken down and rebuilt almost unchanged. The junction of old and new work is marked by new pilasters. On both sides of the new bay there are pedimented niches: a new feature. The statues within these, shown in one of Scott's drawings, never came about. The original sides of the chapel had been stuccoed and, judging from Waterhouse's remark about the defective condition of the chapel, the stucco may have been in bad shape. Its removal revealed rough brickwork, never intended to be exposed. Scott wanted to face these elevations in stone, judging, perhaps correctly, that this is what Wren would have wanted to do (see p. 60).[226] Scott did not have his way on this point: the fellows liked the look of the old brick and, by what must have been a remarkable amount of labour (and at considerable expense), it was made presentable by filling in all the gaps with coloured mortar and then superimposing the regular grid of false pointing that appears today.[227]

---

224 Gavin Stamp, *An architect of promise: George Gilbert Scott junior (1839–1897) and the late Gothic revival* (Donington, 2002).
225 Letters from Scott to the College are in the Pembroke Architectural Archive; the College's letters to Scott are in the RIBA Collection at the Victoria & Albert Museum (SC/CA/PC/).
226 Letter of 14 June 1879, Scott to Prior (Scott corr/16 in Pembroke College Architectural Archive).
227 Letter from Prior to Scott, dated 13 March 1880 (RIBA Collection SC/CA/PC/206). See also Stamp, *Architect of promise*, 154.

78. George Gilbert Scott junior, with his wife, Ellen (née King-Sampson). Scott moved in artistic circles, as his eighteenth-century costume here may suggest. (Carte de visite, National Portrait Gallery / W M Clarke, c.1872)

Internally, the new sanctuary is a distinct space, separated from the body of the chapel by a screen pierced by a grand central arch. Here, coupled pilasters against the north and south walls, and paired columns on each side support an entablature from which the arch springs (Fig. 80). As Stamp observes, it is the fineness of the materials that give this ensemble its special character: the pilasters are of stone, but the columns are formed of massive monoliths of Seravezza marble, brought from the Apennines and worked in London by Farmer & Brindley. The transport and working of these columns caused a good deal of anxiety and delay; Scott was justly proud of the result. The columns are given bronze bases and set on plinths of black Dent marble. All this introduces a quite new note of richness and colour into the chapel. The central section of the original communion rails was set between the bases of the new columns (Figs 79, 80).

In his correspondence with the college, Scott makes the obvious practical point about the division of the chapel into two compartments, namely that:

> The design of the ceiling of the Chapel is such that it would be impossible to extend it without destroying its symmetry. I therefore propose to introduce an arch on the line of the present East wall, separating the body of the Chapel from the altar-space. The ceiling by this plan will not be interfered with.

His only mention of his sources is that, 'The details & proportions of this arch I have studied from some similar arches in St Paul's Cathedral.'[228] These arches can be readily identified:[229] they fill the last (westernmost) bays of the nave arcades on either side, framing the entrances to the chapels (the Chapel of St Michael and St George and the Morning Prayer Chapel) to north and south. These arches are identical in design to that used at Pembroke, except that at St Paul's Wren used Composite capitals for the columns and pilasters (as elsewhere on the pilasters of the nave arcades), whereas Scott remained faithful to the Corinthian order of Pembroke chapel. What he does not say in his letter is that the arch he is proposing to introduce is a Serliana, following, though on a more imposing scale, Wren's Serliana of the east end of the chapel.

Scott may also have had other considerations in mind when devising this arch. 1881, the year in which the chapel extension was completed, also saw the publication of his *An essay on the history of English church architecture*, an erudite volume in which we find him deeply absorbed in the design of the earliest buildings of the Christian church. In a lengthy discussion, he derives the division of the earliest Saxon churches into two compartments from that of the Roman basilica, the wide chancel arch of the former being 'the successor of the triumphal arch of the basilica.'[230] And further,

> In the basilica the holy table was provided with curtains, which were drawn during the recital of the prayer of consecration ... The curtain gave rise to the ... baldachino ... It was a very natural change to substitute for the four supports ... which carried this veil or curtain ... four pillars of marble surmounted by arches bearing a domed roof.[231]

---

228 Letter of 17 January 1879, Scott to Prior (Scott corr/7 in Pembroke College Architectural Archive).
229 By Gordon Higgott (personal communication).
230 George Gilbert Scott, *An essay on the history of English church architecture* (London, 1881), 47.
231 Ibid., 9.

It is difficult not to be reminded by these passages of both the new arch and the four marble columns in Pembroke chapel.

The panelling of the original east wall (that is, on either side of the reredos), together with its carving, was moved without alteration into the new sanctuary. Its side walls (north and south) were given new panelling, adorned with carving taken from the side walls of the original east end: there would have been more than enough. The panelling of the sides of the old east end was thus not altered, but its decorative carving obviously had to be made good. This was done by insertion of new cartouches and festoons, following accurately the pattern of those in the stalls (like those of Fig. 44) and thereby unifying the enlarged body of the chapel.

Comparison of Scott's survey drawing of the original east end interior (Fig. 53) with the present east end shows that he made substantial alterations to the reredos in creating his new sanctuary (Fig. 57). In the original east end, as in the body of the chapel, there was a Corinthian entablature above the panelling, the top of which ran just below the window sills. The triangular pediment of the reredos rose above this, while its pilasters reached down to floor level. As already pointed out (p. 92) the arrangement was pleasing in its order and simplicity. Scott retained this arrangement of the panelling in the new sanctuary and in order to do so had to raise the sill of the east window by 14 inches to allow for three new steps at the east end.[232] A drawing of his proposals for the interior of the east end (Fig. 79) shows that he also initially intended to leave the reredos in its original state, with the pilasters reaching to floor level and the pediment intruding only slightly into the window space. However, he must have decided that the reredos would then appear insignificant in the setting of his new arch, and therefore raised it by just over 47 inches, by inserting pedestals below the pilasters. The pedestals break forward slightly from the new panelling inserted between them and are panelled, with bolection moulding (Fig. 57).[233] The bottom edge of the reredos, originally at floor level, was now level with the top of the altar table and, whereas previously the painting had filled all that was visible of the reredos, from the altar table to the bottom of the architrave (Fig. 53), there was now much empty space. Scott filled this by inserting below the painting a row of three small inset carvings and by introducing above it a wholly new band of carving running the full width of the reredos. Based mainly on leaves and flowers,

---

232 This is confirmed by comparison of Scott's survey drawing of the east end of the chapel before his alterations (SCGGJ[13]87) with the drawing showing his proposed changes (SCGGJ[13]93), both in the RIBA Collection.

233 Scott might have been influenced here by the engraving in Serlio, Book IV, folio 150r (V Hart and P Hicks, *Sebastiano Serlio on architecture* (New Haven and London, 1996), vol. 1, 303) of a structure that could be adapted for diverse functions, 'especially in order to ornament a picture above an altar'. In this reredos-like design, the pilasters are shown with pedestals below.

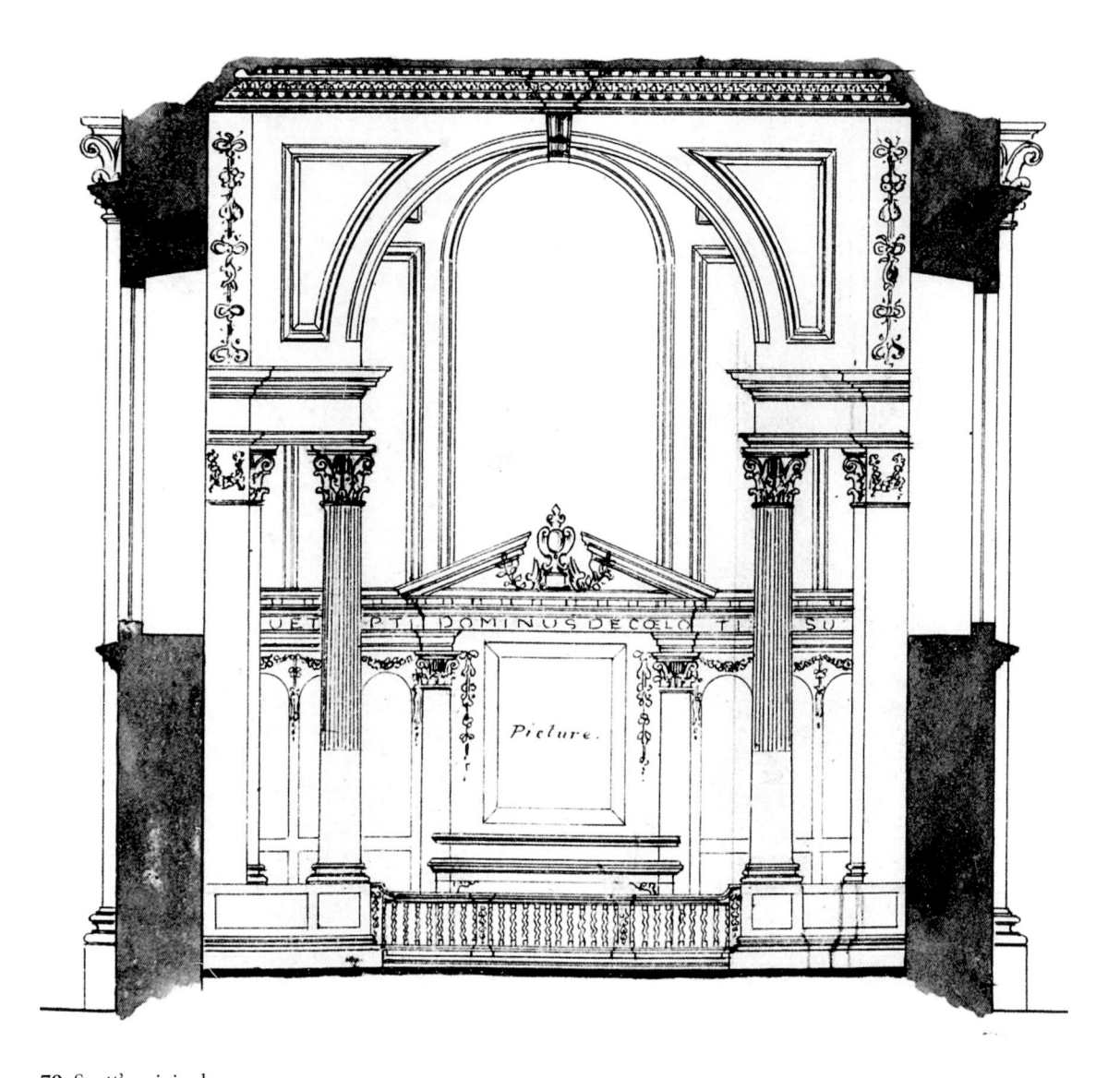

79. Scott's original scheme for the new east end, with the reredos retained at its original level (compare with Fig. 57). (RIBA Library Drawings and Archives Collections, SCGGJ[13]93.)

80. (right) General view of the chapel, looking east end, with Scott's arch. (*Country Life.*)

naturalistically carved and deeply undercut, this is work of considerable skill: notably more florid and realistic than the original carving in the east end and reminiscent of the style of Grinling Gibbons. Two large wheat-ears are prominent and would have had no place in the original carving. Apart from these consequences, raising the reredos causes its top to intrude substantially (and, as might be thought, unfortunately) into the east window space.

New plasterwork in the sanctuary follows closely in style that of the original chapel. The original east end (as Scott's drawing shows) had panels containing crossed palm branches above the side lights of the east window; these are also present in the new sanctuary but are probably copies.

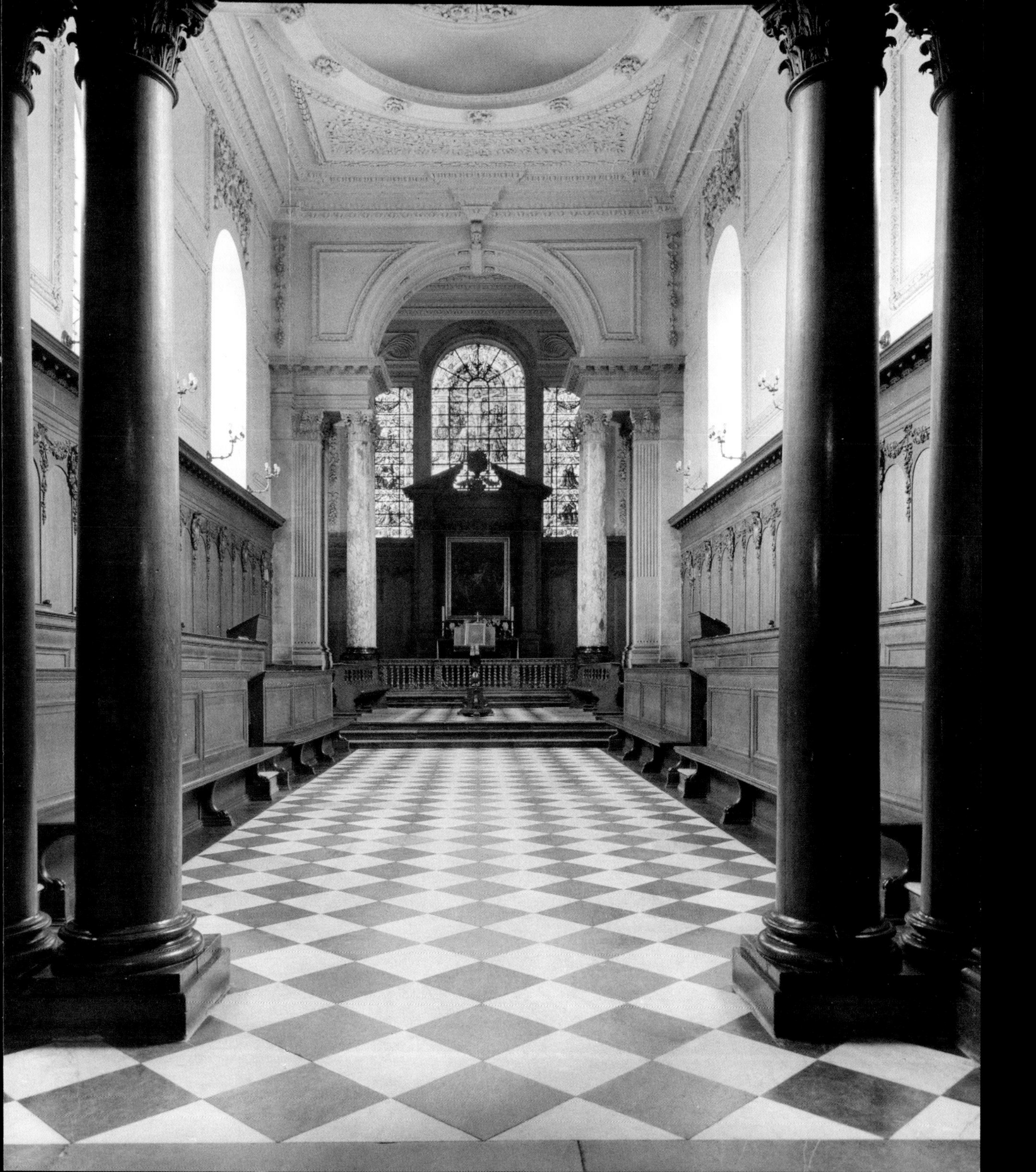

The piscina from the old chapel had survived and Scott found a home for it on the south wall of the sanctuary. He devised a new setting for it, to be carved, apparently, in stone, in Decorated Gothic style,[234] but in the event it was accommodated in a simple rectangular hole, cut in the panelling.

Although Scott had largely saved Wren's chapel, he was not committed to preserving the interior in its original decorative state. One of his drawings for the interior proposes a statue in a niche in the north wall of the sanctuary (presumably to be matched on the south wall). A Latin inscription (as far as can be made out, Psalm 102, verses 20–21) was also suggested, carved or painted on the fascia of the architrave above the panelling and running around both the body of the chapel and the new sanctuary. More radically, a sketch in the College archives sets out proposals for a somewhat startling programme of Biblical scenes that would have included both stained glass in all of the windows, and paintings on all of the rectangular panels between the side windows. Happily (as it now seems), none of this came about, partly, perhaps, because building the new sanctuary took longer than expected and the College was anxious to get the chapel back into use, but also because, with much other building work (to Scott's designs) going on at the same time, the College was findings its resources strained.

In addition to extending the chapel, Scott made extensive alterations to the cloister. This was reduced in width by the introduction on the west (street) side of a row of small rooms (one to serve as a vestry) and new staircases giving access to the rooms above. The existing staircases and their enclosing structures at each end of the cloister (see p. 109) were removed and new arches introduced in their place. These alterations required the chapel door to be shifted eastward (compare Figs 73 and 4) and the door to the organ loft to be moved westward.[235] Doorways from the cloister, giving access to the new rooms, were based on a doorway in Nevile's Court at Trinity College.[236]

---

234 Drawing SCGGJ [13] 99 in the RIBA Collection.
235 The position of the original door to the organ loft is indicated both in the plaster of the chapel interior and in a narrow, arched doorway (now at the back of a cupboard) in an adjacent first-floor room on C staircase.
236 RIBA Collection, SC/CA/PC325.

APPENDICES

Appendix 1: The burials in the vault

Inscriptions on the coffins in the chapel vault were taken by Jayne Ringrose on 20 September 1999, and compared with those taken by Ellis Minns (c.1941), recorded in PCA, MS. C omicron.

1st coffin (at the south end of vault): Matthew Wren.
   Depositum / Rev. in Christo patris / MATHÆI Episc. ELIEN. / Qui obijt xxiiii Aprilis A.D. mdclxvii / Ætat. Suæ LXXXII

2nd coffin: Matthew Wren, eldest son of Matthew Wren.
   Depositum / Matthaei Wren R.P.D.D. Matthaei / Episcopi Eliensis primogeniti / Iacobo Duci Eboracensi / Regiae Classis Praefecto / a Secretis / Qui. / Praelio nauali cum Batauis inito / Vulnere Obijt Iun: An: Dñi 1672 / Ætatis Suæ 430

3rd coffin: Robert Mapletoft, Master.
   DEPOSITVM / ROBERTI MAPLETOFT S.T.P / DECANI ELIENSIS & / MAGISTRI AULÆ PEMBROCHIANÆ / DENATI AVG. 20 1677 / ÆTATIS SVÆ 68.

4th coffin: Charles Wren, son of Matthew Wren
   DEPOSITVM: / CAROLI: WREN: MATTH: EPJ: / ELIENS: FILII: NATV: TERTJJ: / qui:OBJJT:DIE MAJJ / AN:DNI:1680 / ÆTAT:SVÆ:43

5th coffin: Thomas Wren, son of Charles Wren
   DEPOSITUM:THOMIÆ. / WREN:CAROLI:FILIJ

6th coffin: No inscription. Minns notes 'certainly that of William Moses' (Master).

7th coffin: Nathaniel Coga, Master.
   Nathanael Coga S.T.P. et Custos / hujus Collegii obijt pr. id. Jan. / An . Dom . MCDXCIII.

8th coffin: Thomas Brown, Master.
   Depositum / Thomæ Brown / S.S.T.P. / C.C: / Obijt IX Martij 1706 / Ætatis Suæ 60.

9th coffin: Roger Long, Master.
   ROGERVS LONG S.T.P. / hujus Collegii Custos / obijt 16 Dec. 1770 anno ætatis 90

Caskets containing the ashes of four modern fellows stand on a modern shelf running the length of the vault, raised on brick pillars. The inscriptions on these are:
   Aubrey Leonard Attwater Died 11th July 1935 Aged 43 years
   H.G.C. / 1869–1935 [H. G. Comber]
   E.H.Minns 1864–1953
   John Trevor Spittle / Scholar Fellow and President / of this College / 10 May 1886–7 September 1958.

Minns noted that bones found under the cloister *c*.1928 had been placed in the vault. A wooden box on the south end of the shelf bears a metal plate reading 'Found 14 Feet N of NW angle of Chapel head under W Wall of College, Feet to E August 1922'.

Appendix 2: The Pembroke Old Library

Twenty five years after the new chapel was finished Pembroke's old chapel was converted into the College's library (initially the New Library, now the Old Library), which essentially became a seventeenth-century room. This has yet to receive the attention it merits; for present purposes all that need be said is that at the west end a Serliana or Venetian window replaced the Gothic window of Figure 2, new windows of late seventeenth-century pattern were inserted on the north and south sides, and a new ceiling was created. The work was completed by 1690.

The most noteworthy feature of the room is the splendid plaster ceiling, the work of Henry Doogood.[237] This is entirely different in style from the chapel ceiling: the four elements (air, earth, fire and water) are represented here and images of the hunt abound. Doogood was at this time pre-eminent among the London plasterers. He had a long-standing involvement in Wren's works and had been plasterer for thirty-two of the City churches, often working with John Grove senior. There are no records to show who designed the Old Library. For the ceiling, Attwater suggested that, given his long association with Doogood, Wren may have been responsible for the design.[238] One might, indeed, reasonably speculate that Wren may have been consulted about the design of the room as a whole. The architectural work involved would not have been great and much could have been left to the craftsmen. Wren's son, it may be noted, came into residence at Pembroke as a fellow-commoner in 1691, and Wren's brother-in-law, William Holder, a former Pembroke fellow, was among the chief benefactors paying for the conversion of the old chapel.

The room is panelled. All but one pair of the original projecting bookcases have been dismantled but their ends survive, re-set between the windows. They are embellished with small, finely carved friezes (Fig. 81), full of naturalistic foliage, flowers and birds, occasionally with the botanically improbable motif of leaves or strands of berries emerging (cornucopia-fashion) from the centre of flowers. The most striking feature of their decoration, however, is that above the friezes are small cartouches in auricular style, their swelling lobes and scrolls reminiscent of those in the cartouches of the chapel stalls.

---

237 Payment to Doogood for work in the Old Library is recorded in PCA.
238 Aubrey Attwater, *Pembroke College, Cambridge* (Cambridge, 1936), 81

APPENDICES

81. The Old Library, Pembroke College, carving on one of the bookcase ends. The style of the naturalistic frieze below is markedly different from that of the cartouche above, with its grotesque mask at top. This pattern is repeated, with variations, on all of the bookcase ends. (Pembroke Architectural Archive.)

82. Old Library, carving at the east end, detail of the cartouche. As in the chapel prayer desk, the design includes a multiplicity of elements. (Pembroke College Architectural Archive.)

Grotesque masks, part animal, part human, some partly concealed, some of striking ugliness or ferocity, are uniformly present at the top of these cartouches and sometimes as the bottom as well.

The combination of the naturalistic 'classical' friezes with the auricular grotesques is reminiscent of the sort of hybrid design that occurs in the chapel. There is another example in the Old Library. At the east end of the room there is a reredos-like structure, with a finely carved naturalistic frieze, and above it a broken pediment in which is placed a large cartouche, with free-floating festoons on each side (Fig. 82). The composition is strongly reminiscent of the east end of the chapel and may, indeed, have been intended as a reminder that the room was once a chapel. The cartouche immediately engages attention: grotesque animal heads at top and bottom mirror those on the cartouche above the chapel reredos, while the gaping mouth of the 'frog-mouth' helmet pursues the same theme.[239] The vigorously

239 The frog-mouth helmet calls to mind the auricular cartouches with elaborate scroll decoration and frog-like grotesque masks carved under the two niches on the east end of Peterhouse chapel, Matthew Wren's other Cambridge chapel. The ashlaring of this end of Peterhouse chapel is said to have been completed in 1665, the date of completion of Pembroke chapel. Could the cartouches be Pearce's work, and might the frogs (*Rana*) be a pun on Wren's name?

131

swirling carved curves and the writhing foliage above, coupled with the grotesques, are all in auricular style, yet the carver has also included (to left and right of the coat of arms) some small naturalistically carved flowers and two small lambrequins.

The college records are silent on the name of the wood-carvers who worked in the Old Library. The small friezes of the bookcases, like the festoons at both Pembroke and Emmanuel chapels, are controlled, conservative pieces, well within Cornelius Austin's scope. The grotesques of the bookcase cartouches might call to mind those of the chapel cartouches but, in both conception and carving, are altogether too crude to be Pearce's work. The carving at the east end, of much higher quality, could more plausibly be attributed to him, but on stylistic grounds seems more likely to have been carved in imitation of his work.

Appendix 3: Stained glass: the twentieth century

Although Scott's proposals for stained glass were not carried out, it was too much to expect that, in late Victorian times, it could be indefinitely excluded. The London firm of Burlison and Grylls was apparently the first to be approached by the College and there are detailed drawings by them in the College Architectural Archive, for the east window and one of the side windows.[240] These proposals were not adopted, but the idea was not abandoned and stained glass was eventually installed in the east window in 1906, designed and executed by Godfrey Wood Humphry.[241] He must have obtained the commission through being the brother-in-law of Isabella Lucy Humphry, who wished to commemorate Sir George Gabriel Stokes, her father. Stokes was one of the great mathematical physicists of the nineteenth century, Lucasian Professor of Mathematics from 1849 until 1903, President of the Royal Society, fellow of Pembroke and, for a few months before his death, Master.

Apart from the central Crucifixion, the windows commemorate eight benefactors of the college and, less prominently, Stokes. In all three windows the figures are placed in a Classical framework, embellished with laurel wreaths, ribbons, numerous attendant putti and much charming detail. A description is given in the caption to Figure 84.

240 The drawings are undated but are stamped 'Burlison & Grylls, 23 Newman Street, Oxford Street', which was their address from 1868 (when the firm started) to 1907.
241 Humphry usually worked in partnership with Gilbert Percival Gamon (Gamon & Humphry, 52 Grafton Street, Fitzroy Square, London) and the Pembroke window may be their joint work. However, Eric Milner-White, writing about modern stained glass in Cambridge (*Cambridge Review*, 48, (1927), 179–80), attributes the Pembroke window to Humphry alone, describing him as 'a sincere and rare master'.

APPENDICES

83. Detail of the left-hand window, with Sir Robert Hitcham and Sara Lonsdale; at the bottom, dog at left, macaw at right.
(Ian Fleming, 2009)

133

APPENDICES

84. The east window. In the central light the dominant feature is a Crucifixion. To the left, kneeling at the foot of the cross, is the Foundress of the College, Mary de St Pol, in heraldic robes,. She holds a model of the old chapel (part of her original College) and her other foundation, Denny Abbey, is shown above; her arms are displayed on the adjacent column. Opposite her, appropriately, is Matthew Wren, holding the model of the chapel. His mitre and crozier are to hand; the arms of Ely appear on his cope and the cathedral itself is also depicted. This window was given by Mrs Isabella Lucy Humphry in memory of her father, George Gabriel Stokes, and he and her gift are recorded in an inscription at the bottom left, largely obscured by the reredos.

The side windows, which show other benefactors, were inserted at the expense of the College. On the left, from top to bottom, we see Henry VI (shown with Soham Church, the tithes of which he gave to the College); Sir Robert Hitcham (see p. 52), depicted with Framlingham Castle, his gift to the College; and Sara Lonsdale, from whom came a valuable bequest (including Barham Hall, seen in the background) in memory of William Pitt. An informal note is struck by a small lap dog nearby, nestling under a blanket (see Fig. 83). At the top right is Laurence Booth, an early Master of Pembroke who secured for the College the gifts of Henry VI. He built the Library over the medieval hall and planted saffron in the garden (both shown) and was later Archbishop of York, the Minster and Bootham Bar of that City both being depicted. Below him kneels William Smart, alderman of Ipswich, who, in the sixteenth century gave the College valuable manuscripts, one of which lies on the ground beside him; the church of St Mary the Tower at Ipswich (where he is buried) is shown, as is his wharf. Finally, at the bottom of this right-hand light, comes William Moses (Master, 1655–60), responsible for securing the Hitcham bequest, with which Hitcham Building (seen in the background) was erected. All are shown with their arms. Stokes' arms are displayed at the bottom of both side windows. This description is based on that of Sir Ellis Minns, archaeologist and fellow of the College, deeply versed in its history.

The windows are full of charming detail. An attractive but unaccountable feature (perhaps purely decorative) is the presence of a number of birds, mostly of exotic species and in part readily identifiable. In the side windows are two brilliantly coloured South American macaws, the blue Hyacinth Macaw to the right and perhaps a Scarlet Macaw to the left (there is no wholly red macaw such as is shown; the Scarlet Macaw should have some yellow and blue plumage on its wings). In the centre light, to the left, there is what is perhaps best identified as a jacamar, again from South America, while an Asian note is introduced in the form of a monal pheasant (perhaps the Chinese monal) at right. There is also in this window, from Australia, a lyre bird with its characteristic tail. These exotic species are balanced by the presence in the right-hand light of two smaller, more sombrely coloured birds, perhaps European or even British: a species of curlew and some kind of sandpiper (perhaps a stint). I am much indebted to Nick Davies for the identification of all these. (Ian Fleming, 2009)

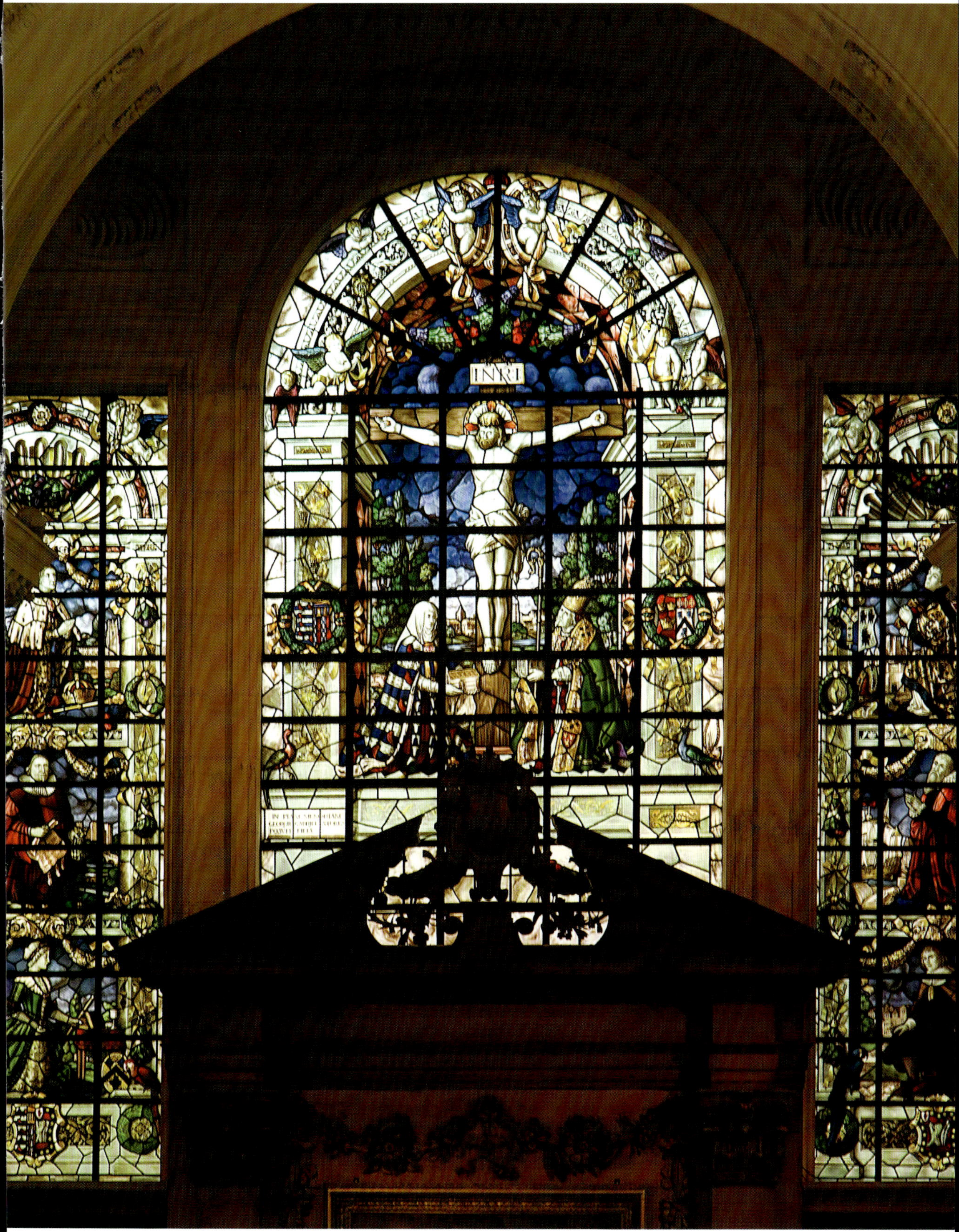
INRI

BIBLIOGRAPHY OF WORKS CITED

Attwater, Aubrey, *Pembroke College Cambridge Society Annual Gazette*, 7 (1933), 17–19.
—, *Pembroke College, Cambridge: a short history* (Cambridge, 1936).

Basford, Kathleen, *The green man* (Ipswich, 1978).
Beard, Geoffrey, *Craftsmen and interior decoration in England, 1660–1820* (Edinburgh, 1981).
Beard, Geoffrey and Cherry A Knott, 'Edward Pearce's work at Sudbury', *Apollo*, 151 (April 2000), 43–8.
Belcher, J and J Macartney, *Later Renaissance architecture in England* (London, 1901).
Bennett, J A, *The mathematical science of Christopher Wren* (Cambridge, 1982).
Berliner, Rudolf, *Ornamentale Vorlageblätter des 13 bis 18 Jahrhunderts* (Leipzig, 1925); reprinted edn Rudolf Berliner and Gerhart Egger (Munich, 1981).
Birch, Thomas, *The history of the Royal Society of London* (London, 1756).
Bolton, A T and H D Hendry (eds), *The Wren Society*, 20 vols (Oxford, 1924–43).
Bowett, Adam, *English furniture, 1660–1714* (Woodbridge, 2002).
Building News (3 May 1907). [Survey drawings of Pembroke chapel, made by W H MacLucas].
Bush, Douglas, 'Science and literature', in H H Rhys (ed.), *Seventeenth century science and the arts* (Princeton, 1961).
Bushell, W D, *Hobson's Conduit* (Cambridge, 1938).

Campbell, J W P, *Building St Paul's* (London, 2007).
—, 'Sir Christopher Wren, the Royal Society and the development of structural carpentry 1660–1710' (unpublished PhD thesis, University of Cambridge, 2000).
—— and A Saint, 'The manufacture and dating of English brickwork 1600–1720', *Archaeological Journal*, 159 (2002), 170–193.
Carter, Edmund, *The history of the University of Cambridge: from its original, to the year 1753* (London, 1753).

Chainey, Graham, 'The lost stained glass of Cambridge', *Proceedings of the Cambridge Antiquarian Society*, 79 (1990), 70–81.
Colvin, Howard, *A biographical dictionary of British architects, 1600–1840*, 4th edn (New Haven and London, 2008).
—, 'The building', in McKitterick, *The making of the Wren Library*, 28–49.
—, (ed.), *The history of the King's works*, 6 vols (London, 1963–82).
—, 'Letters and papers relating to the rebuilding of Combe Abbey, Warwickshire, 1681–1699', *Walpole Society*, 50 (1984), 248–309.
—, *The Sheldonian Theatre and the Divinity School*, 2nd edn (Oxford, 1974).
—, 'Thorpe Hall and its architect', in *Essays in English architectural history* (New Haven and London, 1999) 158–78.
—— and H Oswald, 'The bishop's palace, Lichfield', *Country Life*, 116, (30 December 1954), 2312–15.
Cooper, Charles Henry, *Memorials of Cambridge* (Cambridge, 1866).
Cooper, Trevor (ed.), *The journal of William Dowsing: iconoclasm in East Anglia during the English Civil War* (Woodbridge, 2001).

Davies, C S L, 'Conspiracy, kinship and preferment in the Interregnum and Restoration: the Brunsells and Holders of Nottinghamshire', *Midland History*, 31 (2006), 1–17.
Dircks, Rudolf (ed.), *Sir Christopher Wren, A.D. 1632–1723: bicentenary memorial volume* (London, 1923).
Downes, Kerry, *The architecture of Wren*, 2nd edn (Reading, 1988).
—, *English Baroque architecture* (London, 1966).
—, *Sir Christopher Wren: an exhibition selected by Kerry Downes at the Whitechapel Art Gallery* (London, 1982).
—, *Sir Christopher Wren: the design of St. Paul's cathedral* (London, 1988).

Esterly, David, *Grinling Gibbons and the art of carving* (London, 1998).
Eustace, Katharine, 'Pearce, Edward', *Oxford Dictionary of National Biography* (Oxford, 2004).
Evelyn, John, *Sylva* (London, 1664).

Fincham, Kenneth, 'According to ancient custom: the return of altars in the Restoration church of England', *Transactions of the Royal Historical Society*, 13 (2003), 29–54.
Foster, J E (ed.), 'The diary of Samuel Newton, alderman of Cambridge (1662–1717)', *Cambridge Antiquarian Society Octavo Publications*, 23 (1890), 18–20.
Fürst, Viktor, *The architecture of Sir Christopher Wren* (London, 1956).

Geraghty, Anthony, *The architectural drawings of Sir Christopher Wren at All Souls College, Oxford* (Aldershot, 2007).
—, 'The "dissociation of sensibility" and the "Tyranny of intellect": T.S. Eliot, John Summerson and Christopher Wren', in Frank Salmon (ed.), *The persistence of the classical: essays on architecture presented to David Watkin* (London, 2008).
—, 'Wren's preliminary design for the Sheldonian Theatre', *Architectural History*, 45 (2002), 275–88.
Griffiths, A V, '"The print in Stuart Britain" revisited', *Print Quarterly*, 17 (2000), 118.
Grimstone, A V, 'The vault under the college chapel', *Pembroke College Cambridge Society Annual Gazette*, 74 (2000), 33–36.
Gunnis, Rupert, *Dictionary of British sculptors 1660–1851* (London, 1968).
Gunther, R T, *The architecture of Sir Roger Pratt* (Oxford, 1928).

Harris, J, S Orgel and R Strong, *The king's Arcadia: Inigo Jones and the Stuart court* (London, 1973).
Hart, V and P Hicks (eds), *Sebastiano Serlio on architecture*, vol. 1 (New Haven and London, 1996).

Higgott, Gordon, 'The fabric to 1670', in Keene, Burns and Saint, *St Paul's*, 171–90.
—, 'The revised design for St Paul's cathedral, 1685–90: Wren, Hawksmoor and Les Invalides', *Burlington Magazine*, 146 (2004), 534–47.
—, 'Varying with reason: Inigo Jones's theory of design', *Architectural History*, 35 (1992), 51–77.
Howarth, David (ed.), *Art and patronage in the Caroline courts* (Cambridge, 1993).

Inskip, Peter, 'Emmanuel College chapel: reordering via restoration', *Emmanuel College Magazine*, 87, (2004–5), 55–81.
Intelligencer, The, 2 October 1665 (no 80), 945; reprinted in Willis and Clark, *University of Cambridge*, vol. 1, 621.

Jardine, Lisa, *On a grander scale: the outstanding career of Sir Christopher Wren* (London, 2002).
Jeffery, Paul, *The City churches of Sir Christopher Wren* (London, 1996).
Jervis, Simon, 'A 17th-century book of engraved ornament', *Burlington Magazine*, 128, (1986), 893–903.
—, *The Penguin dictionary of design and designers* (Harmondsworth, 1984).

Keene, D, A Burns and A Saint (eds), *St Paul's: the cathedral church of London, 604–2004* (New York and London, 2004).
King, Peter, 'Matthew Wren, Bishop of Hereford, Norwich and Ely, 1585–1667' (unpublished PhD thesis, University of Bristol, 1969).

Le Pautre, Antoine, *Les Oeuvres d'architecture d'Anthoine Le Pautre* (Paris, 1652; reprinted Farnborough, 1966).
Loggan, David, *Cantabrigia illustrata* (Cambridge, 1690).

McKitterick, David (ed.), *The making of the Wren Library, Trinity College, Cambridge* (Cambridge, 1995).

Meadows, P M, 'Sir Christopher Wren and Pembroke Chapel', *Georgian Group Journal,* 4 (1994) 55–7; reprinted in *Pembroke College Cambridge Society Annual Gazette,* 68 (1994), 25–9.

Milner-White, Eric, 'Modern stained glass in Cambridge', *Cambridge Review,* 48 (21 January 1927) 179–80.

Minns, E H, 'The Wrens' chapel', *Pembroke College Cambridge Society Annual Gazette,* 20 (1946), 9–14.

—— and M E Webb, 'Pembroke College chapel, Cambridge: Sir Christopher Wren's first building', in Dircks, *Sir Christopher Wren,* 229–232.

Newman, John, 'Laudian literature and the interpretation of Caroline churches in London', in Howarth, *Art and patronage in the Caroline courts,* 168–188.

Ogilby, John, *The entertainment of his most excellent majestie Charles II, in his passage through the city of London to his coronation* (London, 1662).

Pacey, Arnold, *Medieval architectural drawing* (Stroud, 2007).

Parry, Graham, *Glory, Laud and honour: the arts of the Anglican counter-reformation* (Woodbridge, 2008).

——, *The seventeenth century: the intellectual and cultural context of English literature, 1603–1700* (London, 1989).

Penny, Nicholas, *Catalogue of European sculpture in the Ashmolean Museum, 1540 to the present day,* vol. 3 (Oxford, 1992).

Pevsner, Nikolaus, *Cambridgeshire,* 2nd edn (Harmondsworth, 1970).

——, *Wiltshire* (Harmondsworth, 1963).

Phillimore, Lucy, *Sir Christopher Wren, his family and his times* (London, 1881).

Physick, John, 'Edward Pierce II', in Jane Turner (ed.), *The dictionary of art* (New York and London, 1996), vol. 24, 753–4.

Plot, Robert, *Natural history of Stafford-shire* (Oxford, 1686).

Poole, Rachel, 'Edward Pierce, the sculptor', *Walpole Society,* 11 (1922–3), 33–45.

Redworth, Glyn, *The Prince and the Infanta* (New Haven and London, 2003).

Ringrose, Jayne, 'Matthew Wren makes his will', *Pembroke College Cambridge Society Annual Gazette,* 67 (1993), 21–26.

Royal Commisssion on Historical Monuments, *An inventory of the historical monuments in the City of Cambridge* (London, 1959).

Scott, George Gilbert Jr, *An essay on the history of English church architecture* (London, 1881).

Sekler, Eduard F, *Wren and his place in European architecture* (London, 1956).

Simon, Jacob, *The art of the picture frame* (London, 1996).

Soo, Lydia M, *Wren's 'tracts' on architecture and other writings* (Cambridge, 1998).

Spittle, Denys, 'Wall-paintings at Pembroke College, Cambridge', *Transactions of the Ancient Monuments Society,* 16 (1969), 109–114. (A shortened version of this paper appears in *Pembroke College Cambridge Society Annual Gazette,* 39 (1965), 10–12.)

Stamp, Gavin, *An architect of promise: George Gilbert Scott junior (1839–1897) and the late Gothic revival* (Donington, 2002).

Stevenson, Christine, 'Occasional architecture in seventeenth-century London', *Architectural History,* 49 (2006), 35–74.

Stubbings, Frank, *Emmanuel College chapel, 1677–1977* (Cambridge, 1977).

Summerson, John, *Architecture in Britain 1530–1830,* 9th edn (New Haven and London, 1969).

——, 'Christopher Wren: why architecture?', in *The unromantic castle and other essays* (London, 1990).

——, *Inigo Jones* (Harmondsworth, 1966).

——, 'Inigo Jones', in *The unromantic castle and other essays* (London, 1990).

——, 'The mind of Wren', in *Heavenly mansions and other essays on architecture* (London, 1949).

——, *Sir Christopher Wren* (London, 1953).

Tipping, H Avray, *Grinling Gibbons and the woodwork of his age* (1648–1720) (London, 1914).

Toplis, G 'The sources of Jones's mind and imagination' in Harris, Orgel and Strong, *The king's Arcadia*, 61–3.

Trevor-Roper, Hugh, 'Little Pope Regulus: Matthew Wren, Bishop of Norwich and Ely', in *From counter-reformation to Glorious Revolution* (London, 1992), 51–71; first printed as 'Matthew Wren', *Pembroke College Cambridge Society Annual Gazette*, 60 (1986), 14–32.

Turner, S J, 'Edward Pierce I', in Jane Turner (ed.), *The dictionary of art* (New York and London, 1996), vol. 24, 752–3.

Walpole, Horace (ed.), *Anecdotes of painting in England . . . collected by the late Mr George Vertue* (Twickenham, 1762–71).

Watkin, D J (ed.) *Sale catalogues of libraries of eminent persons*, vol. 4, Architects (London, 1972).

Webb, Geoffrey, *Wren* (London, 1937).

Whinney, Margaret, *Sculpture in Britain 1530–1830* (Harmondsworth, 1964).

—— and Oliver Millar, *English art 1625–1714* (Oxford, 1957).

Willis, Robert and John W Clark, *The architectural history of the University of Cambridge* (Cambridge, 1886).

Wittkower, Rudolf, *Architectural principles in the age of humanism*, 5th edn (London, 1998).

——, 'Inigo Jones, man of letters', in *Palladio and English Palladianism* (London, 1974).

Worsley, Giles, *Classical architecture in Britain* (New Haven and London, 1995).

——, *Inigo Jones and the European Classicist tradition* (New Haven and London, 2007).

Wren, Christopher Jr (ed.), *Parentalia, or memoirs of the family of the Wrens* (London, 1750; reprinted Farnborough, 1965).

Zülch, W K, *Entstehung des Ohrmuschelstils* (Heidelberg, 1932).

INDEX

Note that many entries are gathered under the heading 'Pembroke College chapel'

All Saints church, Sudbury 67
All Souls College, Oxford, drawings 30, 35, 43, 77
Andrewes, Lancelot 7, 8
Arkesden, Essex 26, 117
Aubrey, John 22
auricular style 70, 86–8, 96–7, 98, 130
Austin, Cornelius 1; master joiner 79–82; wood-carving at Emmanuel College 90; wood-carving at Pembroke College 90–1, 96, 98, 132

baldachino 124
basilica, Roman 124
Beard, Geoffrey 78, 105
Belcher, J & J Macartney 23
Billopps, Richard and William 1, 57, 79–81, 90
Book of friezes 70, 86–7, 97, 102, 115
Bos, Cornelius 67, 88
Bowett, Adam 100
Brunsell H 81, 82
Buckingham, Duke of 8
Burlison & Grylls 132
Bush, Douglas 89–90

Campbell, James 41
Charles, Prince of Wales and king; execution 10; Matthew Wren's association with 8, 9, 13 n.; Spain, visit to 8
Charles II 12; coronation arches 25, 38, 116
Chatsworth, Derbyshire 26, 39
Christ's College, Cambridge 23, 26 n.
City churches, London 7, 35, 51, 74, 86, 100, 105, 130
Clare College, Cambridge, urns 67

Clarendon House, Piccadilly, London 105
Cleere, Richard 78
Coga, Nathaniel 3 n., 79–82, 105, 129
Coleshill House, Berkshire 52, 78
Colvin, Howard 21
Combe Abbey, Warwickshire 39, 70
communion rails 74, 93, 115
communion table, position of 74
Coysevox, Antoine 118

Dobson, William 24
Doogood, Henry 105, 130
Downes, Kerry 12, 45, 46, 70, 71
Dowsing, William 11, 71 n.
Dugdale, William 1
Dunster Castle, Somerset, doorcases 37

Eliot, T S 23 n.
elm wood 84
Eltham Lodge, stone carving 70
Ely House, London 107, 112
Emmanuel College, Cambridge, chapel 20, 21, 24, 26, 28 n., 61, 63, 70, 90, 103
 cost 115
 craftsmen 114–15
 model 39
 Pembroke chapel, comparison with 113–15, 118
 plasterwork, cost 105–6
 stalls 76; designed by Pearce 76
 wood-carving 78, 86, 90, 97, 100; Pearce's role in 115
Esterly, David 82, 93
Evelyn, John 22, 84

Fantuzzi, Antonio 88
Farmer & Brindley, masons 123
Ferguson, Robert 89 n.

Fincham, Kenneth 74
Fisher, Geoffrey 32 n., 38–9, 94
Flory, James 108, 115
Framlingham church, Suffolk, organ 71 n.
Franck, Mark 59
Fuller, Isaac, commemorated in Rome 26; portrait of Edward Pearce 24

Geraghty, A 23 n., 35, 44
Gerbier, Balthazar 8–9, 38
Gibbons, Grinling 67, 78, 81, 87, 126
grotesques 85, 86, 88–9, 96–7, 131
Grove, John 103–6, 115, 130
Grove, John Jr 105–6
Grumbold, Robert 27, 57, 58 n., 63

Hampstead Marshall, Berkshire 39
Hampton Court, urns 68
Hardwick endowment 6
Higgott, Gordon 32 n., 34, 35, 36, 43, 76, 94, 107
high-Anglicanism 6, 10, 74
Hitcham, Sir Robert 52, 109
Hobson's Conduit 31, 55
Holder, William 20–1, 130
Hooke, Robert 22
Horseheath Hall, Cambridgeshire 25, 39
Humphry, Godfrey Wood 132
Hutton, Thomas 59

Jackson, George 59
Jones, Inigo 9, 24, 32, 86
 Banqueting House, London 9, 23
 commemorated in Rome 26
 Pembroke chapel, influence on design 37, 51, 113
 numerical ratios in designs 32–4

140

Queen's Chapel, St James's
  Palace 23, 32, 42, 51, 92
St Paul's cathedral 9, 30, 32, 42, 44
St Paul's church, Covent
  Garden, London 23, 32
Somerset House chapel 23

Kilian, Lukas 88
King, Peter 7 n.
Kingston Lacy, Dorset 52, 116

lambrequin 66–7, 87, 101–2, 117, 132
Laud, archbishop 9, 10, 74
Lemercier, Jacques 70
Le Pautre, Anthoine 109
Le Pautre, Jean 103
Lichfield, Bishop's Palace 26, 37, 70
Loggan, David, engraving of
  Pembroke College 3, 5, 11, 27,
  31, 66, 109, 110
Long, Roger 55 n., 129

Mapletoft, Robert 1, 79–82, 112, 129
May, Adrian 108
May, Hugh 23, 38, 70, 108
Meadows, Peter 12 n., 21, 107
Merchant Taylors' School, London 7
Mills, Peter 27, 38–9, 116
Minns, E H 29, 39, 91, 129, 134

Ogilby, John 38–9

Pacey, Arnold xi, 64, 68, 69
Palladio, Andrea 21, 44, 48, 113
Parentalia 3–4; Pembroke chapel,
  Matthew Wren's gift of 4, 6; not
  attributed to Wren 4, 6, 20, 119
Pearce, Edward 24–6
  Bishop's Palace, Lichfield,
    Staffordshire 26, 37, 70
  capitals 70, 94; drawing of
    37, 70, 94

cartouche, drawing of 88
commemorated in Rome 26
designer 37, 114, 117
draughtsmanship 68, 117
drawing, Pembroke chapel
  29–34; attribution to Pearce
  35–9
Dunster Castle, doorcase 37
Emmanuel College chapel,
  work at 26, 76, 100, 115
funeral monuments 26
grotesques 89
initials in vault 57–8, 79
motifs 117; sources of 88
originality, possible lack of
  117–8
plasterwork, possible role in 103
portrait 24–5
St Paul's cathedral, master
  mason at 26
scale bars 37
stalls, drawing for 76–8
stone carving 65–70
Sudbury Hall 38, 67, 78
Thorpe Hall, staircase 38, 116
triumphal arches, designed by
  38, 116
urns, carved by 65–9
wall drawings 64–9
Wolseley Hall, staircase 100
woodcarving 86–9, 94–8
Wren, Christopher, association
  with 4, 26, 116, 117; bust of
  117–18
Pearce, Edward (senior) 24
Book of friezes 68, 70, 86–7, 97
decorative painter 24; work at
  Wilton House 24
Inigo Jones, association with
  24, 37
urn, engraving of 68–9
Pearson, John 1

Pembroke College chapel
altar 74
ante-chapel 71; paving of 108
architect, appointment of 29,
  37–9
brickwork 59–61, 122; contract
  for 59
capitals, interior 80, 82, 94–6
cartouches 83–8; symbolic
  meaning 89; of reredos 96–7
ceiling 71, 103–6, 124
cherubs 85, 89
Classical style 23; error in 62
cloister 53, 109, 128; staircases
  in 109, 128
columns, interior 76, 80, 82,
  83, 123
communion rails 73, 82, 92,
  98–100, 124
consecration 112
construction, haste in 45, 60,
  61, 66, 83
contracts (see *brickwork* and
  woodwork)
Corinthian order 41, 43, 70,
  94–5
cost 6
craftsmen 114–5
cupola 45, 52
description, general 16–19
design, lack of unity in 45;
  weaknesses of 121
dimensions 42, 46, 52–4
documentation, paucity of 3, 58
drawing, preliminary, of N.
  elevation 29–34; attribution
  to Pearce 35–7
drawings, wall 64–5, 66, 69
east end, interior 91–2, 125–6
east front, 49–51, 62
Emmanuel College chapel,
  comparison with 113–15

INDEX

foundation stone 59
geometry in design 53–4
grotesques 85, 86, 87, 96–8
interior, plan 73–4; ambience 75
lambrequins 66–7, 69, 101–2
lectern 100
misericords 91
model 39–45, 59
oculus, in organ loft 71–3
organ 71 n.
organ loft 18, 71
paintings, Scott's proposed 128
panelling 75, 91
panels, exterior 60–2
paving 21, 73, 80, 83, 106–8
pilasters 18, 48, 123, 125
pilaster bases 43–4
pilaster capitals 70, 94–6
pilaster strips 29
piscina 128
plasterwork 101–6; ceiling 103–5; palm branches 126; wall decorations 101–2
ratios in dimensions 33–4, 53
reredos 82, 91, 92, 93–7, 125–6
roof structure 41–2
sanctuary, new 122, 123
satyr profiles 85, 87–8
Scott's alterations 19, 53, 121–8
screen 76
Serliana, at east end 49, 91, 113; Scott's 124
sources of the design 32, 46–52
stained glass 128, 132–5
stalls 75–9; attributed to Pearce 79
stone carving 63–70; wall drawings for 64–5, 66, 69
stucco 61, 122
symbolic intent 12–13
urns 65–9, 102

vault 2, 12, 55–8, 110–11; burials in 56, 129; graffiti in 56–8, 79
vestry 111
west front 46–8, 61–2
windows 42, 51
wood-carving 82; in body of chapel 83–9, 90–1; clawed feet 78; at east end 91–101, 125–6
woodwork, contract for 79–81
Pembroke College, Ivy Court 27, 28, 63; Hitcham building 27, 38
Pembroke College, old chapel 3, 91 dimensions 11; idolatrous images, destroyed 11; Laudian arrangement of interior 11; piscina 128
Pembroke College, Old Court 27, 109
Pembroke College, Old Library 27, 130–2
Pembroke College, St Thomas' Hostel 28
Penny, Nicholas 118
Peterhouse, Cambridge, chapel 9, 74, 113
Pevsner, Nikolaus 9, 113
Phillimore, Lucy 10
Phillips, Andrew 77
Phillips, Henry 78
Pratt, Sir Roger 25, 38, 39, 52, 78, 105

Quarles, Charles 71 n.
Queen's House, Greenwich 105

Ringrose, Jayne 9 n., 12, 89 n., 129
Royal Society 21–2

St Andrew's, Holborn, London 78
St Clement Danes, City of London 103
St Edmund King & Martyr, City of London 35–6

St John, Stanmore, Middlesex 51
St Katherine Cree, City of London 41
St Lawrence Jewry, City of London 35–6
St Mary, Tarrant Hinton, Dorset 98
St Paul's cathedral 22, 32, 70, 73, 94, 124
St Stephen, Coleman Street, City of London 100
St Stephen, Walbrook, City of London 100
Sampson, William 57, 81, 82
Sancroft, William 20, 74
Sandford, Francis 1
Scott, George Gilbert Jr 53, 65, 109, 121–2
  correspondence, with Pembroke College 31, 122, 124
  Pembroke chapel, drawings of 4, 17, 92, 110, 126; extension of 121–7
Serliana 18, 49, 62, 124
  symbolic significance of 49–51
Serlio, Sebastiano 46, 61, 125 n.
Sheldon, Gilbert 74
Sheldonian Theatre, Oxford 3, 22, 39, 49, 74, 114
Sorbonne chapel, stone carving 70
Spittle, Denys 65, 66
stalls 75–9
Stamp, Gavin 122
St John, Oliver 38
Stearne, Edward 59
Stokes, Sir George Gabriel 53 n., 132
Stubbings, Frank 61
Sudbury Hall, Derbyshire 26, 38, 67, 78, 97, 115, 117
Summerson, Sir John 22, 23

Talman, John 26
Talman, William 26, 39
Temple of the Sibyl, Rome 46
Thamar, Thomas, organ builder 71 n.

INDEX

Thorpe Hall, Northamptonshire 27 n., 38, 116
Thurloe, John 38
Tipping, H A 84
Toplis, G 32, 34
Trevor-Roper, Hugh 7 n.
Trinity College, Cambridge; library 58, 63, 81, 90; doorway 128
twist-turning 99–100

Venetian window (see *Serliana*)

Wallis, John 22
Waterhouse, Alfred 121, 122
Webb, Geoffrey 7, 23
Webb, John 23, 37, 86
Webb, M E 29, 39
Whinney, Margaret 117
Willis, Thomas 22
Wilton House, Wiltshire 24
Winchester College, Hampshire 26, 100, 115
Winde, William 39
Wisbech Castle, Cambridgeshire 38
Wolseley Hall, Staffordshire 26, 100
Worsley, Giles 48, 49, 51
Wren, Anne (d. of Sir Christopher Wren) 82
Wren, Sir Christopher 2, 3–4, 20–2, 39, 45–6, 92, 113–14, 115
  buildings, early, appraised 23, 45
  bust of 117–18
  drawings, pilaster base 43; St Paul's cathedral 30
  models, use of 39, 41
  Paris, visit to 112, 113
  paving, notes on 21, 107–8
  Pearce, association with 26, 116, 118
  Pembroke chapel, designer of 20–1, 38, 44, 113; not attributed to 4, 6, 20, 119
  Professor of Astronomy, Oxford 3, 21
  scientific interests 22
Wren, Christopher (brother of Matthew Wren) 7, 74,
Wren, Christopher, Jr (son of Sir Christopher Wren) 3, 46 n.
Wren, Francis (father of Matthew Wren) 7
Wren, Matthew 1, 41, 59, 60, 83, 89
  bishop 9, 10
  Cambridge University, power in 13
  chapel plate, bequest of 6, 112
  chaplain, to Andrewes 8; to Charles, Prince of Wales 8
  character 7, 10
  consecrates chapel 112
  court, association with 8–9
  cushions 112
  funeral 1–2
  high-Anglicanism 7, 10
  impeachment 10
  imprisonment 10
  Inigo Jones, possible association with 9
  Pembroke chapel, donor of 1, 3, 6, 10–11, 12–13
  Pembroke College, undergraduate & fellow of 7
  Peterhouse, Master of 9
  portrait 7
  Spain, visit to 8
  unpopularity 10
  wealth 10
  will 1, 10, 12, 112
Wittkower, Rudolf 32–4
wood-carving, executed off-site 78

143